The God Who Hears

"In 2015 I published a little book on *Praying the Bible*. Before and since, I have taught on this subject more than 600 times. The exceptional feature of Tom Pennington's book is that—more than in any other book on this subject (including my own) that I've seen—he gives you 31 passages of Scripture to read and then shows you several paragraphs of how *he* prayed from each of them. He doesn't just explain how to pray the Bible and provide a few brief examples; he demonstrates it for you in detail 31 times. Then he leaves plenty of room at the end of each chapter to write your own prayer based on those verses. Use this book for a month and you will know how to pray the Bible."

Donald S. Whitney, Professor of Biblical Spirituality, John H. Powell Professor of Pastoral Ministry, and Director of the Center for Biblical Spirituality at Midwestern Baptist Theological Seminary, Kansas City, MO. Author of *Spiritual Disciplines for the Christian Life*, *Praying the Bible*, and *Family Worship*

"Christians today greatly need to recapture the devotional spirit that made our forebears strong in Christ. Tom Pennington's *The God Who Hears* is a terrific resource both to develop and enrich the daily habit of reading God's Word and prayer. His book is thoroughly consistent with the best of the Reformed tradition, at the heart of which was always the worship of God. May our generation recover the spirit of devotional worship, and may this book spark a flame in the hearts of many readers."

Richard D. Phillips, Senior Minister, Second Presbyterian Church, Greenville, NC

"Throughout the ages, God's people have always been a praying people. Pastor Tom Pennington helpfully puts the focus of prayer where it should be, in the Word. Word-saturated prayer, as the Lord himself taught, is the model for bringing praise and petitions to the Father. You will be blessed by this short, clear, biblical devotional on praying Word-centered prayers."

Brooks Buser, President, Radius International

"In *The God Who Hears*, Dr. Tom Pennington gives rich pastoral and biblical insight and invaluable practice to advance both greater worship through prayer and greater Christian maturity in prayer. From the heart of a pastor and the passion of a discipler, Tom gifts church leaders and members a path to access and honor 'the God who hears.' I commend this book to all who aspire to commune with God and lead the people of God in prayer and through prayer. He is worthy to be sought!"

Harry Walls III, Executive Pastor, Elder, Stonebridge Bible Church, Brentwood, TN

The God Who Hears

31 Days of Reading and Praying Scripture

TOM PENNINGTON

THE WORD UNLEASHED

SOUTHLAKE, TEXAS

The God Who Hears: 31 Days of Reading and Praying Scripture (Second Edition)
Copyright © 2025 by Tom Pennington

Published by © *The Word Unleashed*
Address: PO Box 96077, Southlake, TX 76092
Website: www.thewordunleashed.org
Email: listeners@thewordunleashed.org

The Word Unleashed is a ministry of Countryside Bible Church.
Address: 250 Countryside Ct., Southlake, TX 76092
Website: www.countrysidebible.org

Cover Image at Vecteezy.com
Cover Layout by Jeremy Jessup
Typeset in Novel Pro by Lance Burroughs

Unless otherwise indicated, all Scripture quotations are taken from the
New American Standard Bible®, © 1960, 1962, 1963, 1968, 1971, 1972,
1973, 1975, 1977, 1995 by the Lockman Foundation. Used by permission.
(www.Lockman.org)

All rights reserved. No part of this book may be reproduced or transmitted
in any form or by any means—electronic, mechanical, digital, photocopy,
recording, or any other—except for brief quotations in printed reviews,
without the prior permission of the publisher.

Hardcover ISBN – 9798988509868

Printed in Canada

> "The righteous cry, and the LORD hears
> And delivers them out of all their troubles."
>
> PSALM 34:17

*To God who hears prayer,
and to whom all men come*

—

*"O You who hear prayer,
To You all men come."*

Psalm 65:2

Acknowledgments

The second edition of *The God Who Hears* only exists because of the help of many dear friends and co-laborers. Lance Burroughs conceived this edition, carried it through, and gave it life. He and Matthew Carrington bore the brunt of the editorial work for the content of the first edition, all of which has been retained in the second. Vickie Pier, Megan Schuler, and Martha Koomar spent several weeks proofreading and meticulously working through the final typeset.

As always, I am indebted to the elders of Countryside Bible Church, with whom I have served over 20 years. They have generously and graciously given me time each year to focus on writing.

Finally, I am profoundly grateful to my wife, Sheila, for her partnership in life and ministry. Her daily support, wise counsel, and spiritual encouragement make me a better man and minister.

Ultimately, I thank our Lord Jesus Christ for the privilege and joy of serving the people of His church—those for whom He bled, died, resurrected, and ascended.

Contents

Preface to the Second Edition *xv*

Preface to the First Edition *xxv*

31 Days of Reading and Praying Scripture[1]

1 – The Sovereign Grace of God 1

2 – Thankfulness for God's Goodness 7

3 – The Great High Priest 15

4 – Longing for the New Heaven and Earth 23

5 – The Lord Our Shepherd 29

6 – The Surpassing Value of Knowing Christ 35

7 – The Incarnation of the Eternal Son of God 41

8 – Our Redeemer Lives 47

9 – The Gospel According to the Scriptures 53

10 – Celebrating the Lord's Sustaining Power 59

11 – Bowing Before the Throne of God 67

12 – The Sinner's Need of the Cross 73

13 – Chosen and Called by God 79

14 – Sacrificial Worship of God 85

15 – Treasuring the Word of God 91

16 – Redemption in Christ Jesus 97

17 – God's Forgiving and Redeeming Love 103

18 – The Light of the World 109

19 – The Grace of God in Salvation 117

20 – The Messiah's Kingdom 123

21 – Christ's Prayer for His Own 129

22 – There Is No Other God 137

23 – The Nearness of Yahweh God 145

24 – Jesus' Authority to Forgive Sins 153

25 – Praise the Lord! 159

26 – The Righteousness of Christ 165

27 – The Servant of Yahweh 171

28 – The New Birth 177

29 – The Intercession of Jesus Christ 183

30 – No Other Name 189

31 – The Coming of the Son of Man 195

Endnotes 203

Preface

to the Second Edition

William G. T. Shedd, a nineteenth-century American theologian, once said: "[A pastor] ought to study *method* in prayer, and observe it. A prayer should have a plan as much as a sermon."[1]

Shedd's insight about prayer is vital for Christians to understand and implement today. Many pastors are committed to a weekly schedule and practical process for preparing expository sermons. But to their own spiritual malnourishment, they at times neglect a similar model of intense preparation for praying. Equally concerning is that many believers in the evangelical church are plagued by the same disease: an unwavering commitment to daily reading and studying the Bible yet rarely, if at all, praying.

---

1 William G. T. Shedd, *Homiletics and Pastoral Theology* (Edinburgh: Banner of Truth, 1965), 271.

Shedd continues:

> In the recoil from the formalism of written and read prayers, Protestants have not paid sufficient attention to an orderly and symmetrical structure in public supplications. Extemporaneous prayer, like extemporaneous preaching, is too often the product of the single instant, instead of devout reflection and premeditation. It might, at first glance, seem that premeditation and supplication are incongruous conceptions; that prayer must be a gush of feeling, without distinct reflection. This is an error. No man, no creature, can pray well without knowing what he is praying for, and who he is praying to. Everything in prayer, and especially in public prayer, ought to be well considered and well weighed.[2]

The Bible teaches that both public *and* private prayers are imperative for the people of God. Thomas Watson, an English Puritan, wrote that "prayer is ... the soul's breathing."[3] In that brief statement, Watson captures the seriousness of prayer: it is to your spiritual life what breathing is to your physical life! Without prayer, your Christian life can't survive.

As a servant of Christ who has been entrusted to shepherd His sheep at Countryside, for over twenty years I have endeavored to faithfully lead our congregation in

---

[2] Ibid., 217.
[3] Thomas Watson, *The Beatitudes*, in *Discourses*, 2:305.

Preface to the Second Edition

worship on the Lord's day. I have tried to maintain a genuine commitment to the Second Commandment—that God can only be worshiped in the ways He has explicitly commanded in Scripture. In that, I've sought to champion a key doctrinal principle born out of the Reformation known as the *regulative principle of worship*—only the elements Scripture explicitly prescribes are acceptable in worship.

Therefore, our corporate worship service every Sunday morning includes a Scripture reading—we stand together with our hearts directed toward the Lord, and I read a passage from His Word. This practice reflects what God has prescribed in the New Testament: "Until I come, give attention to the *public* reading *of Scripture*, to exhortation and teaching" (1 Tim. 4:13). Paul uses the Greek word translated "give attention," which means to "occupy oneself with, devote or apply oneself to."[4] Here Paul commands Timothy—and every faithful leader in Christ's church—to devote themselves to reading God's Word to God's people on the Lord's day.

In addition to the reading of Scripture, Paul commands *praying* the Scripture—and to do so on the Lord's day together with the body of Christ. In corporate worship, after I read a text of Scripture, I lead the brothers and sisters of Countryside in a pastoral prayer—based on the passage I just read aloud. I'm intentional about

---

4 William Arndt et al., *A Greek-English Lexicon of the New Testament and Other Early Christian Literature* (Chicago: University of Chicago Press, 2000), 880.

letting the Bible provide the template—at times even the exact words—for the prayer.

Our Lord and the first-century church set an example of praying Scripture, specifically praying the Book of Psalms. The New Testament commands believers to sing the Psalms. The apostle Paul gives this instruction to the churches at Ephesus and Colossae (Eph. 5:19; Col. 3:16). And that same command is also for God's people to *pray* the Psalms. Five psalms are identified in the title as "a prayer" (17; 86; 90; 102; 142). Book Two of the psalter is referred to as "prayers"—the conclusion of Psalm 72 says, "The prayers of David the son of Jesse are ended" (v. 20). This is why John Calvin, the sixteenth-century Reformer, taught that even singing the Psalms is prayer. In his commentary on Psalms, Calvin often refers to the Psalms as "prayers." And elsewhere he writes that singing the Psalms is a form of public prayer. So praying the Psalms sets a pattern for praying the whole of Scripture.

In 1 Timothy 2, the apostle Paul gives Timothy two key principles for prayer in the corporate worship of the church. The first principle focuses on the *content* of prayer: it must be Scriptural. He writes, "I urge that entreaties *and* prayers, petitions *and* thanksgivings, be made on behalf of all men, for kings and all who are in authority, so that we may lead a tranquil and quiet life in all godliness and dignity" (1 Tim. 2:1–2). The Greek word translated "urge" means to exhort and encourage. Paul knew prayer was crucial for the Ephesian church and essential in corporate worship. He uses four words (a collection of synonyms) to describe the content of their prayers: "entreaties," "prayers," "petitions," and "thanksgivings." "Entreaties" denotes an "urgent request to meet a need, exclusively addressed to God." "Prayers" is a general word used often in the New Testament for addressing God in prayer. The Greek word for "petitions" speaks of intercessory prayer on someone else's behalf. "Thanksgivings" means to express gratitude. Paul uses those words to capture the richness of prayer and to encourage church leaders to commit to this discipline in corporate worship.

Paul's exhortation about prayer, specifically the four terms he employs, has deep roots in the Old Testament. David offered a prayer of thanksgiving in 2 Samuel 7:18–29. Solomon humbly made a petition to the Lord (2 Chron. 6:14–42). Nehemiah and Daniel also submitted petitions to God (Neh. 9:5–37; Dan. 9:1–19). Likewise, Abraham, Moses, Hannah, Ezra, Jeremiah, and many others prayed to their heavenly Father. So Paul isn't presenting a novel idea about prayer but rather reflecting the rich history of God's people.

In corporate worship, then, the content of prayer must be saturated with Scripture. But for our prayers to reflect the language of Scripture, we must know the Bible and follow the pattern of the Psalms and the prayers of God's people.

The second principle Paul gives to Timothy concerns the *character* of prayer: it must come from a pure heart. He writes, "I want the men in every place to pray, lifting up holy hands, without wrath and dissension" (1 Tim. 2:8). Prayer must have biblical content but also be offered with godly character. Paul desires that corporate prayer come from a pure heart, one that is "without wrath and dissension." The Greek word for "wrath" means a "state of relatively strong displeasure, [with] focus on the emotional aspect, *anger*."[5] "Dissension" denotes a conflict or argument. Paul's point is that acceptable prayer to God must be offered from a repentant heart and a clear conscience. Our hearts must be right with God and with others. So, a holy and righteous character is also essential for effective prayer. Donald Guthrie writes, "Wrong attitudes of mind are as alien to the holy place of prayer as sullied hands. Not merely pure actions but pure motives are essential in Christian worship."[6]

In addition to public prayer in corporate worship, private prayer is a non-negotiable spiritual discipline for every follower of Jesus Christ. Nothing is more foundational to the Christian life than the place and priority of prayer. Martin Luther once said, "As it is the business of

---

5 Arndt, *A Greek-English Lexicon of the New Testament and Other Early Christian Literature*, 720.
6 Donald Guthrie, *Pastoral Epistles: An Introduction and Commentary*, Tyndale New Testament Commentaries 14 (Downers Grove, IL: InterVarsity Press, 1990), 88.

Preface to the Second Edition

tailors to make clothes and of cobblers to mend shoes, so it is the business of Christians to pray."[7] All Scripture testifies to the importance of prayer in a believer's life. It was a daily priority in the lives of our Lord, the apostles, and New Testament church believers. And Jesus Himself desires that His followers practice the same pattern (Matt. 6:9–13).

In this second edition of *The God Who Hears*, all the content from the first has been retained. But I've added a step-by-step guide to help you develop and maintain the discipline of reading and praying Scripture. Like any discipline, it rarely just happens. A careful, well-thought-out plan is helpful—at times even mandatory. To ensure that our prayers are filled with Scripture and foster rich communion and fellowship with our Lord, *we need a plan*. It's my prayer that the plan I've followed in this book will provide a template for you to create your own plan for prayer.

Each of the 31 prayers begins with a title that captures the theme of the selected Scripture and accompanying prayer. Set the title in your mind and ask the Lord to prepare your heart to read His Word.

Next, read the text of Scripture (perhaps several times if it is unfamiliar to you). And then begin to meditate on it—*deliberately choose to think deeply about it*. As you meditate, ask God to grant you *illumination*—first so that you

---

[7] Martin Luther, cited in John Blanchard, *Gathered Gold: A Treasury of Quotations for Christians* (Welwyn, Hertfordshire, England: Evangelical Press, 1984), 227.

can better understand His truth, and second so that you can better practice it.

Then, I've provided a quote from church history to illustrate how Christians from the past have understood and articulated the truth from that passage of Scripture. It is always encouraging to see what other believers have gleaned from accurately interpreting and applying the wisdom of God's Word.

Next, use my pastoral prayer, which is based on the selected text of Scripture, to order your own thoughts and prayer. In my prayer, I've included the meaning and theme of the biblical text, an overview of its structure, some of its language and vocabulary, and usually an appropriate bridge to the gospel of Jesus Christ. I also incorporate entreaties, requests, thanksgivings, and praises—following the teaching of 1 Timothy 2 and other Scriptures.

Finally, I've provided space for you to write your own prayer using that biblical passage—and to offer it to the God who hears. Psalm 34:17 says, "*The righteous* cry, and the LORD hears and delivers them out of all their troubles." I never cease to be amazed at that profound truth! *The Creator God hears the prayers of His people!* In the Old Testament, most English translations of the Bible employ "LORD" in all capital letters for God's sacred, personal, covenantal name. In Hebrew, God's name consists of only four consonants: "YHWH." In English, we pronounce it *Yahweh*. The point is: *Yahweh Himself* hears every word of *your* prayers and delights to respond.

My prayer is that this book will help you seek your heavenly Father in prayer—and to follow the example of believers for millennia in praying *the Scripture*. My desire—and prayer—is that the Spirit of God will use these pages to invigorate your prayer life, that "the word of Christ [will] richly dwell within you" (Col. 3:16), and that you will use God's own Word to express your heart to Him.

Preface

to the First Edition

This is not a book I planned to write. Prayer is intensely personal—even when you are leading others to the throne of grace. My wife Sheila was the first to suggest it. She thought it would be helpful to publish some of my pastoral prayers as a pattern of praying the Scripture. Though I value her input and advice, I was hesitant. But after several others approached me with the same request, I concluded that the Lord might be pleased to use this project for that good purpose.

God demands that we worship Him according to what He has prescribed in Scripture. His revelation, not our own imagination, is the standard. The basic message of the Second Commandment is that God alone determines how He is to be worshiped (Exod. 20:4). Any expression of worship beyond His revealed will is idolatry (Exod.

32:4–5). The Westminster Confession of Faith (21.1) affirms this by stating:

> The acceptable way of worshipping the true God is instituted by Himself, and so limited by His own revealed will, that He may not be worshipped according to the imaginations and devices of men ... or any other way not prescribed in the holy Scripture.

As a minister of God's Word, I have tried to faithfully lead our congregation in biblical worship that takes the Second Commandment seriously. Our worship service every Sunday morning includes a Scripture reading—we stand together and I read a passage of Scripture—because God has prescribed it in His Word. In 1 Timothy 4:13, the apostle Paul writes, "Until I come, give attention to the *public reading of Scripture*, to exhortation and teaching." "Give attention" is an imperative. Paul is not suggesting Timothy read the Scriptures in corporate worship. He commands it.

The public reading of Scripture plays a crucial role throughout the biblical narrative. Moses repeatedly read the law aloud to the nation of Israel (Deut. 31:11–12). Moses' successor, Joshua, read the book of the law to the assembly of Israel (Josh. 8:34–35). Centuries later, Ezra demonstrated the same relentless commitment to the public reading of Scripture (Neh. 8:5–8).

Preface to the First Edition

During our Lord's ministry, it was His custom to read the Scripture to those attending corporate worship in the synagogue (Luke 4:16–21). Paul instructed New Testament churches to publicly read God's Word (Col. 4:16; 1 Thess. 5:27). In the prologue to the Book of Revelation, which was written to churches, the apostle John writes, "Blessed is he who *reads* and those who *hear* the words of the prophecy" (Rev. 1:3; emphasis added). "He who reads" is singular and refers to the church leader. "Those who hear" is plural and refers to the members of the congregation. John expected that when the leaders of the seven churches received his letter, they would read it out loud to their people.

Along with reading Scripture, God also commands us to pray as part of corporate worship (1 Tim. 2:1–2). On Sunday mornings after reading Scripture, I lead the congregation in a pastoral prayer based on the passage just read. Following the pattern of biblical prayers, I let Scripture provide the framework and often even the words for the prayer.

The concept of praying God's Word is most notably found in the Book of Psalms. The entire book provides a divinely intended record and pattern for worshiping God, in prayer and praise. Paul tells the believers in Ephesus to "[speak] to one another in psalms and hymns and spiritual songs, singing and making melody with [their hearts] to the Lord" (Eph. 5:19). He makes the same point in Colossians 3:16, "Let the word of Christ richly dwell within you, with all wisdom teaching and admonishing one another with psalms and hymns and spiritual songs, singing with thankfulness in your hearts to God." In these passages, Paul commands believers to sing and to pray the Psalms.

Many psalms are prayers. Five are specifically identified in the title as a "prayer" (17; 86; 90; 102; 142). Scripture refers to one of the five books of the psalter as "prayers." The conclusion of Psalm 72 says, "The prayers of David the son of Jesse are ended" (v. 20).

Our Lord often prayed using the words of the Psalms. His longest saying on the cross (Matt. 27:46) was a prayer in the words of Psalm 22:1, "My God, my God, why have You forsaken me?" Moments before His death, Jesus prayed, "Father, INTO YOUR HANDS I COMMIT MY SPIRIT" (Luke 23:46)—words taken directly from Psalm 31:5.

New Testament believers prayed the Psalms. Acts 4:23–26 records that the early church lifted "their voices to God with one accord," praying Psalm 2:1–2 and 146:6.

Both the reading and the praying of Scripture are non-negotiable parts of corporate worship. As a pastor, if I neglect either element, I am being disobedient to God and His Word.

In addition to the biblical commands to read and pray Scripture, there is another motive that compels me to go before the throne of God in prayer: He hears me! Psalm

34:17 says, "The righteous cry, and the LORD hears and delivers them out of all their troubles." What a profound reality! The God of the universe hears the prayers of His people. When the redeemed cry out to Him, He truly listens and responds. How encouraging it is to know that our heavenly Father listens to our prayers.

It is my desire that the following prayers will encourage you to pray—and to pray the Scripture. Several collections of prayers have often benefited me. My hope is that the Lord will use these prayers to enrich your prayer life in a similar way, helping you to take prayer more seriously, better organize your prayers, express your heart more clearly, and think more deeply about God and His Word.

This book would never have been published without the contribution of others. I am profoundly grateful to my wife Sheila for her faithful partnership, wise counsel, and unwavering encouragement to use the gifts God has given—"her worth is far above jewels" (Prov. 31:10). Lance Burroughs conceived this book project, carried it through these many months, and now has given it life. He and Matthew Carrington bore the brunt of the editorial work. It is impossible for me to adequately thank the elders who have generously given me time each year to focus on writing. Ultimately, I thank our Lord Jesus Christ for the privilege and joy of serving His church.

Day 1

The Sovereign Grace of God
Titus 3:1–8

—

Preparation
Ask your heavenly Father to prepare your heart to read and pray His eternal Word.

Scripture Reading
The Word of God reads:

> Remind them to be subject to rulers, to authorities, to be obedient, to be ready for every good deed, to malign no one, to be peaceable, gentle, showing every consideration for all men. For we also once were foolish ourselves, disobedient, deceived, enslaved to various lusts and pleasures, spending our life in malice and envy, hateful, hating one another. But when the kindness of God our Savior and His love for mankind

appeared, He saved us, not on the basis of deeds which we have done in righteousness, but according to His mercy, by the washing of regeneration and renewing by the Holy Spirit, whom He poured out upon us richly through Jesus Christ our Savior, so that being justified by His grace we would be made heirs according to the hope of eternal life. This is a trustworthy statement; and concerning these things I want you to speak confidently, so that those who have believed God will be careful to engage in good deeds. These things are good and profitable for men.

Meditation
Deliberately choose to think deeply about what you just read from God's Word. Ask God to grant you illumination so that you can better understand His truth and plan how to practice His truth.

Reflect on Church History
Consider what John Chrysostom (347–407), one of the greatest preachers in the early church, writes about Titus 3:5:

> Strange, isn't it, how we were so drowned in wickedness that we could not be purified? We needed a new birth! For this is implied by "regeneration." For as when a house is in a ruinous state no one places props under it nor makes any addition to the old building, but pulls it down to its foundations and

rebuilds it anew. So in our case, God has not repaired us but made us anew.[2]

Prayer
Use this prayer to help you better organize your own prayer, express your heart more clearly, and think more deeply about God and His Word.

O Father, we thank You for the picture you have drawn in this passage. We thank You for the reminder of what we once were—of what all who are not in Christ still are. We were deceived and in slavery to our sin; we were living in malice toward You and toward others, completely consumed with ourselves.

We thank You that You saved us. You found us in that wretched condition, unable to respond to You and even unaware of our true condition. We were dead in trespasses and sins, but You intervened, in sovereign grace, to rescue us. You were not motivated by anything in us—not by any works we had done, not by anything in our own hands, not by our merit or effort—but rather simply by Your own great heart, because You are compassionate, merciful, and full of grace, and because You loved mankind. Thank You that You have rescued us, that by Your Spirit You have washed us and made us new. At the moment of conversion, You regenerated us.

O God, as grateful as we are for what You did in the past, when You saved us from the penalty of sin, we pray that Your saving work would continue even today, that You would continue to rescue us from the power of sin in our lives. Thank You that sin's power was broken at the cross. May that reality be demonstrated in our lives more and more as sin loses its hold on us and we continue in the path of righteousness.

Father, may we demonstrate the good works You have enabled us to do. As Paul reminds us here, may we be careful, having believed in You, to engage in good deeds. Help us to be respectful toward others who are not in Christ, remembering that we used to be just like them, and would be still, apart from Your grace.

God, we thank You not only for the salvation You wrought in us in the past by saving us from the penalty of sin and for the salvation that is even now at work in our sanctification to save us from the power of sin, but also for our future salvation, when You will save us from the very presence and possibility of sin. We are so grateful that someday we will not even be like Adam was before his fall, but we will be like Christ: completely unable to sin eternally.

We long for that day, but until then may we be faithful to

You. May You work in us so that our walk is worthy of the calling with which You have called us to Yourself.

We pray in the name of our Lord Jesus Christ.

Amen.

Response
Write your own prayer based on the same biblical passage and boldly offer it to the God who hears.

....
....
....
....
....
....
....
....
....
....
....
....
....
....
....
....

The God Who Hears

Day 2

Thankfulness for God's Goodness
Psalm 65

—

Preparation
Ask your heavenly Father to prepare your heart to read and pray His eternal Word.

Scripture Reading
The Word of God reads:

> There will be silence before You,
>   and praise in Zion, O God,
>   And to You the vow will be performed.
> O You who hear prayer,
>   To You all men come.
> Iniquities prevail against me;
>   As for our transgressions, You forgive them.
> How blessed is the one whom You choose

The God Who Hears

and bring near *to You*
    To dwell in Your courts.
We will be satisfied with the goodness of Your house,
    Your holy temple.

By awesome *deeds* You answer us in righteousness,
    O God of our salvation,
        You who are the trust of
            all the ends of the earth
                and of the farthest sea;
Who establishes the mountains by His strength,
    Being girded with might;
Who stills the roaring of the seas,
    The roaring of their waves,
        And the tumult of the peoples.
They who dwell in the ends *of the earth*
    stand in awe of Your signs;
        You make the dawn
            and the sunset shout for joy.

You visit the earth and cause it to overflow;
    You greatly enrich it;
        The stream of God is full of water;
            You prepare their grain,
                for thus You prepare the earth.
You water its furrows abundantly,
    You settle its ridges,

Thankfulness for God's Goodness

> You soften it with showers,
> > You bless its growth.
> You have crowned the year with Your bounty,
> > And Your paths drip with fatness.
> The pastures of the wilderness drip,
> > And the hills gird themselves with rejoicing.
> The meadows are clothed with flocks
> > And the valleys are covered with grain;
> > > They shout for joy, yes, they sing.

Meditation
Deliberately choose to think deeply about what you just read from God's Word. Ask God to grant you illumination so that you can better understand His truth and plan how to practice His truth.

Reflect on Church History
Consider what David Dickson (1583–1662), Professor of Divinity at Glasgow and Edinburgh, writes about Psalm 65:2:

> The hearing and granting of prayer are the Lord's property, and his usual practice, and his pleasure, and his nature, and his glory: "O thou that hearest prayer!"[3]

Prayer
Use this prayer to help you better organize your own prayer, express your heart more clearly, and think more deeply about God and His Word.

Our Father, when we gather with our family and friends, help us to remember these words of David that prompt us to bring You our thanks perpetually, not simply on a special day or special week: we are to celebrate Your goodness every day.

Like David, we celebrate Your temporal goodness to us, all the blessings of this life. And Father, while we do not live in an agrarian society as he did, we acknowledge that these realities are just as true for us as they were in his day. The food we enjoy is a gift from Your hand because You cause the earth to be fruitful and give its abundance. You water it and cause its growth.

Father, we thank You for Your goodness; every good gift we enjoy comes down to us from Your hand (Jas. 1:17). We recognize that Your goodness truly is a witness to You across this earth. As Paul reminds us, Your goodness prompts You to send rain from heaven and fruitful seasons. You graciously satisfy our hearts, and the hearts of all people across this globe, with food and gladness (Acts 14:17).

Lord, we give You thanks for the abundance we enjoy here. But, with David, our hearts turn from the temporal blessings of this life to our spiritual blessings. We thank You for the reality of forgiveness from transgressions.

Thankfulness for God's Goodness

How blessed we are that You have chosen us to draw near to Yourself—so near that You have adopted us as sons and daughters.

You are the God of our salvation in Jesus Christ, and we rejoice in the knowledge that, as much as we enjoy the good things in this life, we will one day dwell in Your presence forever on a new earth where righteousness is at home.

We bless You and thank You for the good things that are ours. Forgive us for failing to thank You and for limiting our thanks—for offering thanksgiving so seldom and with less than our whole hearts.

Lord, You are good, and every good thing comes to us from Your hand through our Lord Jesus Christ, in whose name we pray.

Amen.

Response
Write your own prayer based on the same biblical passage and boldly offer it to the God who hears.

....
....

The God Who Hears

Thankfulness for God's Goodness

Day 3

The Great High Priest
Hebrews 10:11–25

Preparation
Ask your heavenly Father to prepare your heart to read and pray His eternal Word.

Scripture Reading
The Word of God reads:

> Every priest stands daily ministering and offering time after time the same sacrifices, which can never take away sins; but He, having offered one sacrifice for sins for all time, SAT DOWN AT THE RIGHT HAND OF GOD, waiting from that time onward UNTIL HIS ENEMIES BE MADE A FOOTSTOOL FOR HIS FEET. For by one offering He has perfected for all time those who are sanctified. And the Holy Spirit also testifies to us; for after saying,

"This is the covenant
   that I will make with them
After those days, says the Lord:
I will put My laws upon their heart,
And on their mind I will write them,"

He then says,

"And their sins and their lawless deeds
I will remember no more."

Now where there is forgiveness of these things, there is no longer *any* offering for sin.

Therefore, brethren, since we have confidence to enter the holy place by the blood of Jesus, by a new and living way which He inaugurated for us through the veil, that is, His flesh, and since *we have* a great priest over the house of God, let us draw near with a sincere heart in full assurance of faith, having our hearts sprinkled *clean* from an evil conscience and our bodies washed with pure water. Let us hold fast the confession of our hope without wavering, for He who promised is faithful; and let us consider how to stimulate one another to love and good deeds, not forsaking our own assembling together, as is the habit of some, but encouraging *one another*; and all the more as you see the day drawing near.

Meditation
Deliberately choose to think deeply about what you just read from God's Word. Ask God to grant you illumination so that you can better understand His truth and plan how to practice His truth.

Reflect on Church History
Consider what Martin Luther (1483–1546), a German Reformer, writes about Hebrews 10:19–25:

> We "have confidence to enter," for [Christ] himself opened this way for us and at the same time is for us the priest who sympathizes with our weaknesses and is able to help those who are tempted. For this reason, we have no excuse for delaying, since he certainly cannot do more for us than he is doing. For while others can teach and exhort us to cross over, this Christ alone is not only the companion but also the one who leads the way, not only the leader but also the helper, yes, the ferryman.[4]

Prayer
Use this prayer to help you better organize your own prayer, express your heart more clearly, and think more deeply about God and His Word.

Our Father, we are amazed at Your grace toward us in Christ. We thank You, O God, that through the perfect, once-for-all sacrifice of the body of Jesus Christ and His death for sin, You have torn the veil and allowed us into Your very presence.

We thank You that what was once a barrier has, through Christ, been opened for us, and now we can enter Your presence because of what He has done.

We can enter through the torn veil: the beaten, bruised, and bloodied body of our Savior, Jesus Christ. Through Him we gain not merely access, but confident access as those who belong.

We thank You, Father, for such an amazing gift to us in Christ, that through His one offering You have made us right with You. You have perfected forever those who are being sanctified. You have given us such an amazing Savior! I pray that You would produce in us a faith to live by Him.

May Jesus Christ be our great High Priest, our Lamb, our Redeemer, all our desire, our only hope, and our only boast.

May we enter into Him as our refuge and build our lives on Jesus Christ as the foundation of everything. May we walk in Him as the Way, the Truth, and the Life and follow Him as our Shepherd and Guide. May we listen to His instructions—for we are His disciples, and He is our Lord and Master. May we rely on His death on the cross as our only hope of standing before You without being swept away in the flood of Your judgment. And may we daily depend on His intercession for us as our great High Priest, as One who stands before You on our behalf.

Father, thank You that Your great Lamb, Your Sacrifice for sin, has now become the High Priest. Help us to love Him, to follow Him, to obey Him, and to live our lives for Him, in response to the One who has brought us near.

May we constantly draw nearer to You in this life now that we have access into Your presence through Christ, and may we hold fast to our profession of hope, knowing that in Him Your promises are Yes and Amen (2 Cor. 1:20).

I pray that You would help us not to forsake our assembling together, as is the habit of some, but instead to gather and encourage each other in love and good deeds until the day dawns in which our Lord returns.

We pray all these things in Jesus' name.

Amen.

Response

Write your own prayer based on the same biblical passage and boldly offer it to the God who hears.

The Great High Priest

Day 4

Longing for the
New Heaven and Earth
Revelation 21:22–22:7

—

Preparation
Ask your heavenly Father to prepare your heart to read and pray His eternal Word.

Scripture Reading
The Word of God reads:

> I saw no temple in it, for the Lord God the Almighty and the Lamb are its temple. And the city has no need of the sun or of the moon to shine on it, for the glory of God has illumined it, and its lamp is the Lamb. The nations will walk by its light, and the kings of the earth will bring their glory into it. In the daytime (for there

will be no night there) its gates will never be closed; and they will bring the glory and the honor of the nations into it; and nothing unclean, and no one who practices abomination and lying, shall ever come into it, but only those whose names are written in the Lamb's book of life.

Then he showed me a river of the water of life, clear as crystal, coming from the throne of God and of the Lamb, in the middle of its street. On either side of the river was the tree of life, bearing twelve *kinds of* fruit, yielding its fruit every month; and the leaves of the tree were for the healing of the nations. There will no longer be any curse; and the throne of God and of the Lamb will be in it, and His bond-servants will serve Him; they will see His face, and His name *will be* on their foreheads. And there will no longer be *any* night; and they will not have need of the light of a lamp nor the light of the sun, because the Lord God will illumine them; and they will reign forever and ever.

And he said to me, "These words are faithful and true"; and the Lord, the God of the spirits of the prophets, sent His angel to show to His bond-servants the things which must soon take place.

"And behold, I am coming quickly. Blessed is he who heeds the words of the prophecy of this book."

Meditation
Deliberately choose to think deeply about what you just read from God's Word. Ask God to grant you illumination so that you can better understand His truth and plan how to practice His truth.

Reflect on Church History
Consider what John MacArthur (1939–), Pastor-Teacher at Grace Community Church, writes about Revelation 21–22:

> The eternal capital city of heaven, the New Jerusalem, will be a place of indescribable, unimaginable beauty. From the center of it the brilliant glory of God will shine forth through the gold and precious stones to illuminate the new heaven and the new earth. But the most glorious reality of all will be that sinful rebels will be made righteous, enjoy intimate fellowship with God and the Lamb, serve Them, and reign with Them forever in sheer joy and incessant praise.[5]

Prayer
Use this prayer to help you better organize your own prayer, express your heart more clearly, and think more deeply about God and His Word.

Our Father, although it is a wonderful gift from You, this life is a life of shadows. Our brief and uncertain time here reminds us that we were not made for this. You have put eternity in our hearts (Eccl. 3:11), and we are not satisfied by a mere seventy or eighty years (Ps. 90:10).

We thank You that as wonderful as this life can be because of Your work in us through Your Spirit, Your Word, and the church, to the glory of Your Son, this is not all there is for us. We thank You that someday, if our Lord tarries and we sleep in death, we will awake the next moment in Your glorious presence in heaven where You dwell.

Ultimately, our destiny and eternal home is a new earth where righteousness is at home and where everything will be perfect: no hint of the curse, no sign of sin, but only perfect love and joy and Your perfect presence forever.

Father, we look forward to the day when we will see You, however You choose to manifest Yourself but especially in the humanity of Your Son. We thank You that He has a glorified body and that someday we, too, will have a body like His glorious body (1 Cor. 15:35–49; 1 John 3:2). We thank You that in the new earth we will serve You, worship You, and do all that You made us to do, using our minds and being challenged by the work You assign us, all in a perfect environment. Most of all, Father, we thank You we will be without sin and in Your glorious presence.

Longing for the New Heaven and Earth

Lord, forgive us for living as though this life is all there is. Forgive us for being enslaved and captivated by the things of this world, as if they are the things that matter. Remind us, O God, that everything around us will be burned up, completely and permanently destroyed (2 Pet. 3:10–12) and that all that really matters is You and the people You have placed around us. May we spend our lives for the things that matter.

Help us to live in anticipation of our eternal future, enjoying life here, but always looking for that new heaven and new earth in which righteousness is at home (2 Pet. 3:13).

We thank You that we can belong there because of our Lord Jesus Christ, because of what He has done for us, and because we have His righteousness.

It is in His name we pray.

Response
Write your own prayer based on the same biblical passage and boldly offer it to the God who hears.

....
....
....

The God Who Hears

Day 5

The Lord Our Shepherd
Psalm 23

—

Preparation
Ask your heavenly Father to prepare your heart to read and pray His eternal Word.

Scripture Reading
The Word of God reads:

> The LORD is my shepherd,
>> I shall not want.
>
> He makes me lie down in green pastures;
>> He leads me beside quiet waters.
>
> He restores my soul;
>> He guides me in the paths of righteousness
>>> For His name's sake.

Even though I walk through the valley
>of the shadow of death,
>>I fear no evil, for You are with me;
>>>Your rod and Your staff, they comfort me.
You prepare a table before me
>in the presence of my enemies;
>>You have anointed my head with oil;
>>>My cup overflows.
Surely goodness and lovingkindness
>will follow me all the days of my life,
>>And I will dwell in
>>>the house of the LORD forever.

Meditation
Deliberately choose to think deeply about what you just read from God's Word. Ask God to grant you illumination so that you can better understand His truth and plan how to practice His truth.

Reflect on Church History
Consider what Augustine of Hippo (354–430), an early Church Father, writes about Psalm 23:

> I shall not be afraid of evil happenings, because you live in my heart through faith; you are with me now to ensure that when this shadow of death has passed away, I may be with you.[6]

Prayer

Use this prayer to help you better organize your own prayer, express your heart more clearly, and think more deeply about God and His Word.

Father, we are so grateful that You have given us this wonderful psalm that has been such a comfort and encouragement to Your people for three thousand years, and still is to us today as we read these words.

We thank You, O God, that You have revealed Yourself in a way we would never have supposed: You have told us You are our Shepherd—not only collectively, but in a real and personal sense. As the New Testament reveals, You have become our Good Shepherd in the person of our Lord Jesus Christ (John 10:11).

We thank You, O God, that in Him we lack nothing we need. Thank You that You have provided for us not only materially and physically but also spiritually. You alone restore our souls, and You direct us when we have strayed from the right path. You bring us back and lead us again on the path of righteousness, not merely for our sake, but for the sake of Your great name.

When we face the darkest, deepest valleys of this life, even the valley of the shadow of death, we do not need to be afraid because You never leave us. You are always with us as our perfect Shepherd. We are never alone, and we do not have to fear.

A day is coming when we will gather at a great banquet as Your invited guests and celebrate Your victory over Your enemies and ours.

But, Father, the truth that encourages us most is that throughout this life and into eternity Your goodness and Your steadfast love will never leave us. They will pursue us like the hounds of heaven into Your very presence, where we will no longer be merely sheep in Your pasture and guests at Your banquet, but Your sons and daughters who will live in the house You have prepared for us forever!

Thank You for such amazing grace. We ask that in this life You would help us to stay on the path of righteousness, by Your grace, for Your name's sake.

We pray in Jesus' name.

Amen.

Response
Write your own prayer based on the same biblical passage and boldly offer it to the God who hears.

The Lord Our Shepherd

The God Who Hears

Day 6

The Surpassing Value of Knowing Christ
Luke 14:25–33

—

Preparation
Ask your heavenly Father to prepare your heart to read and pray His eternal Word.

Scripture Reading
The Word of God reads:

> Now large crowds were going along with Him; and He turned and said to them, "If anyone comes to Me, and does not hate his own father and mother and wife and children and brothers and sisters, yes, and even his own life, he cannot be My disciple. Whoever does not carry his own cross and come after Me cannot be

My disciple. For which one of you, when he wants to build a tower, does not first sit down and calculate the cost to see if he has enough to complete it? Otherwise, when he has laid a foundation and is not able to finish, all who observe it begin to ridicule him, saying, 'This man began to build and was not able to finish.' Or what king, when he sets out to meet another king in battle, will not first sit down and consider whether he is strong enough with ten thousand *men* to encounter the one coming against him with twenty thousand? Or else, while the other is still far away, he sends a delegation and asks for terms of peace. So then, none of you can be My disciple who does not give up all his own possessions."

Meditation
Deliberately choose to think deeply about what you just read from God's Word. Ask God to grant you illumination so that you can better understand His truth and plan how to practice His truth.

Reflect on Church History
Consider what Leon Morris (1914–2006), a New Testament theologian, writes about Luke 14:33:

> Jesus does not want followers who rush into discipleship without thinking of what is involved. And he is clear about the price. Anyone who comes

to him must *renounce all that he has*. For the third time we have the solemn refrain, he *cannot be my disciple* (26–27). These words condemn all half-heartedness. Jesus is not, of course, discouraging discipleship. He is warning against an illconsidered, fainthearted attachment in order that those who follow him may know the real thing. He wants them to count the cost and reckon all lost for his sake so that they can enter the exhilaration of full-blooded discipleship.[7]

Prayer

Use this prayer to help you better organize your own prayer, express your heart more clearly, and think more deeply about God and His Word.

Our Father, we thank You for the clarity of our Lord's words and his call to discipleship. We thank You for the reminder that to be His disciple, we must rather have Him than anything. Our affection for those we love most in this world must appear like hate compared to the intensity of our love for Jesus. We must be willing to give up everything in this world to gain Christ.

Lord, thank You that there was a point in our lives when You brought us to see not only the desperate darkness of our sin, but the brilliant glory of Jesus Christ, when everything else seemed unimportant and completely lacking compared to the surpassing value of knowing Christ Jesus our Lord (Phil. 3:8).

We thank You, Father, that by a work of Your grace each of us can sing, "I'd rather have Jesus than anything this world affords today."[8] And we can cry out, "Give us Jesus, only Jesus!"

Thank You for showing us that in Him Your wrath was appeased at the cross, that in His death, death was destroyed and You granted us forgiveness and justification—we were declared right before You.

We thank You that since You brought us to know You in Christ, He has daily been faithful to us. He has been our teacher, our sanctifier, our director, our everything. We thank You, O God, that all we need is in Him.

Lord, people we love are going through extreme difficulties in this life; some we know of and many we do not. Remind them that whatever their trouble, Jesus is enough. He alone can truly give them comfort in their distress. They can run to Him and find peace.

When we are tempted, remind us that our only hope is to trust not in ourselves, but in His strength as the only One who has ever completely resisted temptation. Remind us, O God, that even our most extreme difficulties in this life do not equal the trials He endured, and that He is our strength, our shield, and our help.

Father, remind us that ultimately, all we need in this world, even if we lose everything else, is Jesus. Seal that on our hearts.

We pray in Jesus' name.

Amen.

Response
Write your own prayer based on the same biblical passage and boldly offer it to the God who hears.

....
....
....
....
....
....
....
....
....
....
....

The God Who Hears

Day 7

The Incarnation of the Eternal Son of God
Matthew 1:18–25

—

Preparation
Ask your heavenly Father to prepare your heart to read and pray His eternal Word.

Scripture Reading
The Word of God reads:

> Now the birth of Jesus Christ was as follows: when His mother Mary had been betrothed to Joseph, before they came together she was found to be with child by the Holy Spirit. And Joseph her husband, being a righteous man and not wanting to disgrace her, planned to send her away secretly. But when he had

considered this, behold, an angel of the Lord appeared to him in a dream, saying, "Joseph, son of David, do not be afraid to take Mary as your wife; for the Child who has been conceived in her is of the Holy Spirit. She will bear a Son; and you shall call His name Jesus, for He will save His people from their sins." Now all this took place to fulfill what was spoken by the Lord through the prophet: "Behold, the virgin shall be with child and shall bear a Son, and they shall call His name Immanuel," which translated means, "God with us." And Joseph awoke from his sleep and did as the angel of the Lord commanded him, and took Mary as his wife, but kept her a virgin until she gave birth to a Son; and he called His name Jesus.

Meditation
Deliberately choose to think deeply about what you just read from God's Word. Ask God to grant you illumination so that you can better understand His truth and plan how to practice His truth.

Reflect on Church History
Consider what J. C. Ryle (1816–1900), an Anglican bishop of Liverpool, writes about Matthew 1:18–25:

> The name Jesus means "Saviour." It is the same name as Joshua in the Old Testament. It is given to our Lord because "He saves His people from their sins."

The Incarnation of the Eternal Son of God

This is His special office. He saves them from the guilt of sin, by washing them in His own atoning blood. He saves them from the dominion of sin, by putting in their hearts the sanctifying Spirit. He saves them from the presence of sin, when He takes them out of this world to rest with Him. He will save them from all the consequences of sin, when He shall give them a glorious body at the last day. Blessed and holy are Christ's people! From sorrow, cross, and conflict they are not saved. But they are saved from sin for evermore. They are cleansed from guilt by Christ's blood. They are made [fit] for heaven by Christ's Spirit. This is salvation.[9]

Prayer

Use this prayer to help you better organize your own prayer, express your heart more clearly, and think more deeply about God and His Word.

Father, thank you for this simple, straightforward record of the most monumental event in human history.

This passage reminds us of why we so desperately needed Jesus to come into the world: before Your grace, before Christ, we had destroyed ourselves, defiled our souls, and prostituted all Your good gifts to us. We were miserable, vile, and without hope. If we were ever to be rescued, it would only be by Your goodness, undeserved and astonishing, and by the riches of Your amazing grace shown to us in Christ.

Lord, we are grateful that You devised a means in eternity past to rescue us from our sin and guilt, and to restore us to happiness, honor, safety, and peace with You—to reconcile us to Yourself. We bless You that even as this text reminds us, there was only one way, and that was through the Mediator whom You appointed—not just any mediator, but Your own unique, eternal Son, who willingly stepped out of the light of heaven into the darkness of this planet and became one of us (Phil. 2:5–11; 1 Tim. 2:5–6).

We thank You, Father, that the mission You gave Your Son to accomplish—our forgiveness—He embraced willingly and did not fail to accomplish. Rather, on the cross when His ministry was done, when His work of atonement was accomplished, He declared, "It is finished!" (John 19:30). Then He bowed His head in death, only to be raised by You in power on the third day. In His death and in His resurrection, Your law was magnified, Your justice was satisfied, and a foundation was laid for our eternal hope.

We praise You and we bless You for our Lord Jesus

Christ. Help us at Christmas and throughout the year to celebrate Him. Lord, do not let this world's distractions rob us of the reality of the incarnation.

And, Father, open not only our hearts to adore and worship Him but our mouths to confess Him to neighbors, coworkers, family, and friends. O God, give us courage, wisdom, love, and boldness to proclaim His gospel.

We ask it in Jesus' name.

Amen.

Response
Write your own prayer based on the same biblical passage and boldly offer it to the God who hears.

The God Who Hears

Day 8

Our Redeemer Lives
Job 19:23–29

—

Preparation
Ask your heavenly Father to prepare your heart to read and pray His eternal Word.

Scripture Reading
The Word of God reads:

> "Oh that my words were written!
>   Oh that they were inscribed in a book!
> "That with an iron stylus and lead
>   They were engraved in the rock forever!
> "As for me, I know that my Redeemer lives,
>   And at the last He will take His stand on the earth.
> "Even after my skin is destroyed,
>   Yet from my flesh I shall see God;

Whom I myself shall behold,
> And whom my eyes will see and not another.
>> My heart faints within me!
"If you say, 'How shall we persecute him?'
> And 'What pretext for a case
>> against him can we find?'
"Then be afraid of the sword for yourselves,
> For wrath *brings* the punishment of the sword,
>> So that you may know there is judgment."

Meditation
Deliberately choose to think deeply about what you just read from God's Word. Ask God to grant you illumination so that you can better understand His truth and plan how to practice His truth.

Reflect on Church History
Consider what Charles H. Spurgeon (1834–1892), a Baptist pastor, writes about Job 19:

> I am sure the gloom of death is altogether gone now that the lamp of resurrection burns .... Since we know that our Redeemer lives, this shall be our comfort in life—that though we fall, we shall not be utterly cast down. And since our Redeemer lives, this shall be our comfort in death—that though worms destroy this body, yet in our flesh we shall see God.[10]

Prayer

Use this prayer to help you better organize your own prayer, express your heart more clearly, and think more deeply about God and His Word.

Father, our own hearts unite with Job's in eager anticipation and expectation that, though we die, for us death is not final. Though our skin is destroyed, though our bodies are buried and become the food of worms and turn to dust, yet in our flesh we will see You. We thank You that someday our perfected spirits will be united with glorified bodies like the body of our Lord, that we will see You and stand physically in Your presence (Phil. 3:21; Col. 3:10).

Father, we bless You that for us death is not final. It is the last great enemy that Christ our Lord will destroy. It is part of the curse You pronounced on a fallen world. Death itself belongs to You; You are its Sovereign. Through the life and death of the Lord Jesus Christ, You are also victorious over it and the sin that caused it.

He defeated death in His death, and He has brought forth life in His resurrection. Because He has risen, we too shall be raised. We, like Job, O God, know that our Redeemer lives, and at the last, He will take His stand upon the earth and we will see Him.

Lord, forgive us for knowing about the reality of the resurrection, for knowing about the reality of eternity, and living as if this life is all there is. Remind us, O God, that You have put eternity in our hearts: our souls cannot be satisfied with seventy or eighty years. Rather, we long for eternal life, we long for life with You forever.

We thank You that You have made eternal life with You possible in and through our Lord Jesus Christ. Like Job, someday we will be completely vindicated—if not in this life, then certainly in Your presence. In that day, You will declare that we are among those whom You had already declared righteous, not with our own righteousness but with the righteousness of our Lord Jesus Christ.

Until that day, Lord, help us to live with an eye that looks toward eternity, that looks toward the future, that is not earthbound or time-bound (2 Cor. 4:18).

We pray in the name of Jesus, our Redeemer who lives.

Amen.

Response
Write your own prayer based on the same biblical passage and boldly offer it to the God who hears.

Our Redeemer Lives

The God Who Hears

Day 9

The Gospel According to the Scriptures
1 Corinthians 15:1–8

—

Preparation
Ask your heavenly Father to prepare your heart to read and pray His eternal Word.

Scripture Reading
The Word of God reads:

> Now I make known to you, brethren, the gospel which I preached to you, which also you received, in which also you stand, by which also you are saved, if you hold fast the word which I preached to you, unless you believed in vain.

For I delivered to you as of first importance what I also received, that Christ died for our sins according to the Scriptures, and that He was buried, and that He was raised on the third day according to the Scriptures, and that He appeared to Cephas, then to the twelve. After that He appeared to more than five hundred brethren at one time, most of whom remain until now, but some have fallen asleep; then He appeared to James, then to all the apostles; and last of all, as to one untimely born, He appeared to me also.

Meditation
Deliberately choose to think deeply about what you just read from God's Word. Ask God to grant you illumination so that you can better understand His truth and plan how to practice His truth.

Reflect on Church History
Consider what Philipp Melanchthon (1497–1560), a German Reformer, writes about 1 Corinthians 15:

> Paul discusses the resurrection of the dead, the fruit of Christ's resurrection, Christ's kingdom, the power of death, the power of sin, and the power of the law. Second, the occasion for this chapter was the error and wickedness of some Corinthians, who doubted the resurrection of the dead and the immortality of the soul; and he condemns this error with many varied

arguments. He immediately begins his argument without an explicit proposition. And he draws out his argument from the example of Christ in this manner: If Christ has risen, then there is a resurrection of the dead.[11]

Prayer

Use this prayer to help you better organize your own prayer, express your heart more clearly, and think more deeply about God and His Word.

Our Father, we thank You for the gospel, the good news You have declared through Your Son: that there is a way for Your enemies to be reconciled to You, to know You not only as God but as Father.

We thank You for the truths of the gospel. Your eternal Son took on humanity, became like us in every way except for sin, while retaining His deity, and lived among us in perfect obedience to You. Then, according to the Scriptures, He died for our sins. For those hours on the cross, He bore Your justice, Your anger against the sin of everyone who would ever believe in Him.

We thank You that He was buried—proving that He actually died—that He tasted death for every man who would believe in Him. You subjected Him to death—the

One who had only been perfectly obedient to You—so that we, who deserve only death, might know life.

We praise You that You raised Him from the dead on the third day as evidence forever that You had accepted His perfect sacrifice for sin. You did not raise Him as a spirit or a ghost, but in His full humanity: He appeared to many, was touched, ate and drank with them, and then visibly ascended into Your presence where He is, even now, seated at Your right hand until He returns for His own.

Father, we thank You that by Your grace You brought us to hear and understand the gospel, and through that gospel drew us to Yourself so that we responded with repentance for our sins and faith in our Lord Jesus Christ.

We praise You, we thank You, and we love You. We pray that You would give us hearts that long to understand and obey Your Word.

We pray in Jesus' name.

Amen.

Response
Write your own prayer based on the same biblical passage and boldly offer it to the God who hears.

The Gospel According to the Scriptures

The God Who Hears

Day 10

Celebrating the Lord's Sustaining Power
Psalm 104:1–23

—

Preparation
Ask your heavenly Father to prepare your heart to read and pray His eternal Word.

Scripture Reading
The Word of God reads:

> Bless the LORD, O my soul!
>> O LORD my God, You are very great;
>>> You are clothed with splendor and majesty,
>> Covering Yourself with light as with a cloak,
>>> Stretching out heaven like a *tent* curtain.
>> He lays the beams of His upper chambers in the waters;

The God Who Hears

He makes the clouds His chariot;
> He walks upon the wings of the wind;

He makes the winds His messengers,
> Flaming fire His ministers.

He established the earth upon its foundations,
> So that it will not totter forever and ever.

You covered it with the deep as with a garment;
> The waters were standing above the mountains.

At Your rebuke they fled,
> At the sound of Your thunder they hurried away.

The mountains rose; the valleys sank down
> To the place which You established for them.

You set a boundary that they may not pass over,
> So that they will not return to cover the earth.

He sends forth springs in the valleys;
> They flow between the mountains;

They give drink to every beast of the field;
> The wild donkeys quench their thirst.

Beside them the birds of the heavens dwell;
> They lift up *their* voices among the branches.

He waters the mountains from His upper chambers;
The earth is satisfied with the fruit of His works.

He causes the grass to grow for the cattle,
> And vegetation for the labor of man,

So that he may bring forth food from the earth,
And wine which makes man's heart glad,
So that he may make *his* face glisten with oil,
And food which sustains man's heart.
The trees of the LORD drink their fill,
The cedars of Lebanon which He planted,
Where the birds build their nests,
And the stork, whose home is the fir trees.

The high mountains are for the wild goats;
The cliffs are a refuge for the shephanim.
He made the moon for the seasons;
The sun knows the place of its setting.
You appoint darkness and it becomes night,
In which all the beasts of the forest prowl about.
The young lions roar after their prey
And seek their food from God.
When the sun rises they withdraw
And lie down in their dens.
Man goes forth to his work
And to his labor until evening.

Meditation

Deliberately choose to think deeply about what you just read from God's Word. Ask God to grant you illumination so that you can better understand His truth and plan how to practice His truth.

Reflect on Church History
Consider what George Horne (1730–1792), Bishop of Norwich and Dean of Canterbury, writes about Psalm 104:

> This is a hymn, full of majesty and sweetness, addressed to [Yahweh], as Creator of the world. It setteth forth his glory, wisdom, goodness, and power, displayed in the formation of the heavens and earth (1–9), in the various provisions made for beasts, and birds, and for man, the lord of all (10–18), in the revolutions of the celestial bodies, and the consequent interchanges of day and night, of labour and rest (19–24).[12]

Prayer
Use this prayer to help you better organize your own prayer, express your heart more clearly, and think more deeply about God and His Word.

Father, what an amazing celebration of Your creative power!

We thank You, O God, that You have made all things. For Your own pleasure they were created. You have manifested Your majesty and Your power and Your glory all around us. Lord, only our sinfulness and fallen hearts keep us from seeing You everywhere we look, from seeing Your eternal power and divine nature painted across the creation.

Celebrating the Lord's Sustaining Power

Father, we thank You that in Christ You have opened our eyes not only to see the glory of the gospel, but also to see Your greatness in all You have made. We thank You that You sustain this world. When the rain falls, we are reminded that it is Your care for the planet You made and maintain. Remind us that these things are not controlled by impersonal laws, but rather by principles and guidelines You put into place and moment by moment superintend.

Lord, we pray as we look at Your creation, as we see its order and structure, as we see Your care for it all, remind us of Your special care for Your own. Remind us that You have set Your love and care upon us in a way You have not done for this planet, because someday You will destroy it. But for us who love You, Your love and care will continue forever.

We thank You, O God, that You made such love and care possible through the spotless life of our Lord Jesus Christ, and through His death in the place of sinners.

We thank You and bless You in His great name.

Amen.

Response

Write your own prayer based on the same biblical passage and boldly offer it to the God who hears.

Celebrating the Lord's Sustaining Power

Day 11

Bowing Before the Throne of God
Ephesians 3:14–21

—

Preparation
Ask your heavenly Father to prepare your heart to read and pray His eternal Word.

Scripture Reading
The Word of God reads:

> For this reason I bow my knees before the Father, from whom every family in heaven and on earth derives its name, that He would grant you, according to the riches of His glory, to be strengthened with power through His Spirit in the inner man, so that Christ may dwell in your hearts through faith; and that you, being rooted

and grounded in love, may be able to comprehend with all the saints what is the breadth and length and height and depth, and to know the love of Christ which surpasses knowledge, that you may be filled up to all the fullness of God.

Now to Him who is able to do far more abundantly beyond all that we ask or think, according to the power that works within us, to Him *be* the glory in the church and in Christ Jesus to all generations forever and ever. Amen.

Meditation

Deliberately choose to think deeply about what you just read from God's Word. Ask God to grant you illumination so that you can better understand His truth and plan how to practice His truth.

Reflect on Church History

Consider what Charles Hodge (1797–1878), professor at Princeton Seminary, writes about Ephesians 3:20–21:

> Paul's prayer had apparently reached a height beyond which neither faith, nor hope, nor even imagination could go, and yet he is not satisfied. An immensity still lay beyond. God was able to do not only what he had asked, but infinitely more than he knew how either to ask or think. Having exhausted all the forms

of prayer, he casts himself on the infinitude of God, in full confidence that he can and will do all that omnipotence itself can effect. His power, not our prayers nor our highest conceptions, is the measure of the apostle's anticipations and desires. This idea he weaves into a doxology, which has in it more of heaven than of earth.[13]

Prayer
Use this prayer to help you better organize your own prayer, express your heart more clearly, and think more deeply about God and His Word.

Our Father, we rejoice in Your great goodness to us. We thank You that we are named as Your own, that we are Your children, and that we can address You, even as Paul does here, as Father.

Lord, we bow our hearts before You to make great requests of You, which are far beyond what we could ever imagine You would do for us. You have taught us to come boldly in and through Jesus Christ to ask audacious things of You. So, we now make for ourselves the same requests Paul made for the believers in Ephesus.

We pray that each one of us, according to Your great riches and awesome power, may be strengthened with

Your might by Your Spirit in our inner man. Father, we are weak by nature. Even though we belong to You, our resolve quickly melts, our determination suddenly flees, and our courage easily changes to fear. We come asking You to give us the spiritual strength in our souls to know Your will and to do it.

We also pray, O God, that You would allow our Lord Jesus Christ, in and through His Spirit, to dwell within our hearts through faith, so that we who have come to truly know and embrace Him through the gospel would grow in our awareness of His abiding presence. As we walk through each day and go about the responsibilities and tasks of this life, remind us that our Lord is with us.

Finally, we pray that You would allow our understanding of the love Christ has shown us to grow more profound and deep. We ask You to allow His love to be the foundation on which our entire Christian lives grow. As we understand His eternal, electing, saving, redeeming love, may the sins which tempt us, become so much less appealing. May their hold on us diminish, and may we grow in our likeness to Him. As we are filled up with Your fullness, may our character increasingly be an imitation of Your own.

Father, these are huge requests, but we acknowledge, as

Paul did, that You are able to do far more than all that we can ask or think, according to Your power at work in us.

May You receive the glory in Your Son, our Lord Jesus Christ, and in us, His church, both now and in the ages to come.

We pray in Jesus' name.

Amen.

Response
Write your own prayer based on the same biblical passage and boldly offer it to the God who hears.

....
....
....
....
....
....
....
....
....
....
....
....

The God Who Hears

Day 12

The Sinner's Need of the Cross
Romans 3:9–20

—

Preparation
Ask your heavenly Father to prepare your heart to read and pray His eternal Word.

Scripture Reading
The Word of God reads:

> What then? Are we better than they? Not at all; for we have already charged that both Jews and Greeks are all under sin; as it is written,
>
> "THERE IS NONE RIGHTEOUS, NOT EVEN ONE;
> THERE IS NONE WHO UNDERSTANDS,

> There is none who seeks for God;
> All have turned aside,
> > together they have become useless;
> > > There is none who does good,
> > > > There is not even one."
> "Their throat is an open grave,
> > With their tongues they keep deceiving,"
> > > "The poison of asps is under their lips";
> "Whose mouth is full of cursing and bitterness";
> "Their feet are swift to shed blood,
> Destruction and misery are in their paths,
> And the path of peace they have not known."
> "There is no fear of God before their eyes."

Now we know that whatever the Law says, it speaks to those who are under the Law, so that every mouth may be closed and all the world may become accountable to God; because by the works of the Law no flesh will be justified in His sight; for through the Law comes the knowledge of sin.

Meditation

Deliberately choose to think deeply about what you just read from God's Word. Ask God to grant you illumination so that you can better understand His truth and plan how to practice His truth.

Reflect on Church History

Consider what F. F. Bruce (1910–1990), a New Testament scholar, writes about Romans 3:9–20:

> [God's] law brings out men and women's sinfulness but does nothing to cure it. Jews as well as Gentiles, then, have to confess themselves morally bankrupt. If there is any hope for either group, it can be found only in the mercy of God and not in any claim that individuals or nations may try to establish on him. Because of the universal fact of sin, the way of acceptance with God by reason of our works of righteousness is closed—the notice is clearly worded: "No Road This Way."[14]

Prayer

Use this prayer to help you better organize your own prayer, express your heart more clearly, and think more deeply about God and His Word.

Our Father, we approach You with full hearts ready to worship You. This text reminds us of what we were, of who we were, before You found us in Christ.

Your Word takes us back in time to when we didn't know You. It reminds us of when we sat under Your condemnation, under Your judgment, anticipating eternal separation from You because of our personal guilt, our lack of righteousness, and our rebellion against You, our rightful King.

We thank You that this chapter of Romans also takes us back to the cross as it reminds us that our Lord offered Himself for us because of our sin. There was no other way, no other plan in Your great eternal mind and wisdom, to redeem us to Yourself: only the cross.

We bless You that for us the terrible reality in this passage has been removed through the cross—we do not have to anticipate that future day of judgment for our sins because You judged them finally, fully, and ultimately in Christ.

Having satisfied Your justice, You have forgiven us. You have adopted us into Your own family. You have made us Your own children. We know You and the joys of walking with You in this life, as well as the hope of being in Your presence worshiping, serving, and knowing You in deeper and more profound ways for all eternity as we continually experience Your kindness to us in Christ Jesus.

Father, we bless You for the gospel—not only for giving us the good news, but for revealing the bad news that makes the gospel so good.

The Sinner's Need of the Cross

Help us, Lord, to open our minds to see and understand the reality of the good news of the gospel. Change us because of that precious truth which You have revealed in Your timeless, eternal Word.

We pray in Jesus' name.

Amen.

Response
Write your own prayer based on the same biblical passage and boldly offer it to the God who hears.

....
....
....
....
....
....
....
....
....
....
....
....
....
....

The God Who Hears

Day 13

Chosen and Called by God
2 Thessalonians 2:13–17

Preparation
Ask your heavenly Father to prepare your heart to read and pray His eternal Word.

Scripture Reading
The Word of God reads:

> But we should always give thanks to God for you, brethren beloved by the Lord, because God has chosen you from the beginning for salvation through sanctification by the Spirit and faith in the truth. It was for this He called you through our gospel, that you may gain the glory of our Lord Jesus Christ. So then, brethren, stand firm and hold to the traditions which

you were taught, whether by word of mouth or by letter from us.

Now may our Lord Jesus Christ Himself and God our Father, who has loved us and given us eternal comfort and good hope by grace, comfort and strengthen your hearts in every good work and word.

Meditation
Deliberately choose to think deeply about what you just read from God's Word. Ask God to grant you illumination so that you can better understand His truth and plan how to practice His truth.

Reflect on Church History
Consider what Heinrich Bullinger (1504–1575), a Swiss Reformer and theologian, writes about the apostle Paul's words in 2 Thessalonians 2:13–17:

> And he does here very cunningly bring in together the whole sum of the gospel, that is to say, that God has loved humankind, and given to them everlasting consolation, that is Jesus Christ, who is our hope, and has given it to us through his grace, and not for our merits, that is to say, that we might live evermore. He wishes unto them (I say) that the same meek and loving God would comfort their hearts and establish them in all good saying and doing, that is to

say, in all righteousness. For in these two things he comprehends all the offices or duties of a Christian person.[15]

Prayer

Use this prayer to help you better organize your own prayer, express your heart more clearly, and think more deeply about God and His Word.

O Father, we are painfully aware that we live on a fallen planet, in a world that is saturated by sin, that is under Your curse, that is filled with the lies of Your great enemy, Satan. It is a world that groans under the weight of its own sin.

Lord, when we look around us, when we are tempted for a moment to be earthbound people, thinking only about this life and what lies before us here, it is easy for us to become discouraged, disheartened, and even to live in some measure of fear.

We thank You for the reminder You gave the Thessalonian believers through Paul, and that You give us as well: You have already written our spiritual story, and it is not yet complete. We thank You, O God, for the fact that You have set Your love upon us. It would be enough if we could simply be called "beloved by the Lord."

Father, we thank You that You set Your love upon us for a particular purpose. In eternity past You chose us from the beginning for salvation. We thank You that even before our lives began, You set Your love upon us.

We also thank You that when we were living in sin and rebellion, when we were trying to satisfy our own desires—living for pleasure, sin, selfishness, comfort, wealth—there was a moment when You interrupted our lives with the gospel. You brought a copy of Your Word or a preacher, friend, neighbor, or family member to share the truth of the gospel with us. And through that gospel message You called us to Yourself. You gave us faith and repentance and changed us in a moment's time. We became a new creation.

We praise You that You continue to work through the sanctifying influence of Your Spirit as He makes us increasingly like Christ. While we are so far from what we long to be, which is perfectly like Christ, we thank You that we can see we are no longer what we used to be—You have changed us. We take this as a promise for the future when we will be like Christ in every way.

And as wonderful as all these things are, Father, we know that our story has really just begun: You saved us and called us through the gospel so that we might see the glory of our Lord Jesus Christ and gain glorified bodies like His in order to live in His presence forever.

Do not let us forget this truth. Do not let us lose sight of it in this sin-soaked and cursed world. Remind us of our future. Help us to stand firm and to hold to the biblical traditions we received in the Scripture. Until our Lord comes or calls us home, may our Lord Jesus Christ Himself and You, God our Father, who has loved us and given us eternal comfort and good hope by Your grace, comfort and strengthen our hearts in every good work and word.

We pray in Jesus' name.

Amen.

Response
Write your own prayer based on the same biblical passage and boldly offer it to the God who hears.

....
....
....
....
....
....
....

The God Who Hears

Day 14

Sacrificial Worship of God
Mark 14:3-9

Preparation
Ask your heavenly Father to prepare your heart to read and pray His eternal Word.

Scripture Reading
The Word of God reads:

> While He was in Bethany at the home of Simon the leper, and reclining *at the table*, there came a woman with an alabaster vial of very costly perfume of pure nard; *and* she broke the vial and poured it over His head. But some were indignantly *remarking* to one another, "Why has this perfume been wasted? For this perfume might have been sold for over three hundred

denarii, and the money given to the poor." And they were scolding her. But Jesus said, "Let her alone; why do you bother her? She has done a good deed to Me. For you always have the poor with you, and whenever you wish you can do good to them; but you do not always have Me. She has done what she could; she has anointed My body beforehand for the burial. Truly I say to you, wherever the gospel is preached in the whole world, what this woman has done will also be spoken of in memory of her."

Meditation
Deliberately choose to think deeply about what you just read from God's Word. Ask God to grant you illumination so that you can better understand His truth and plan how to practice His truth.

Reflect on Church History
Consider what William Hendriksen (1900–1982), a New Testament scholar, writes about Mark 14:3–9:

> One is prone to commit the error of becoming so filled with admiration for Mary's beautiful deed as to forget that what she did was only a reflection of the Master's own kindness toward her. Consider not only his mercy in saving her but also the tenderness he revealed when in this particular moment he rushed to her defense. After all, he knew that the hour of his own

Sacrificial Worship of God

incomparably bitter suffering was fast approaching. Nevertheless, so deeply did he love his own that, because of his appreciation for what she had done, he was wounded deeply by the unjustified criticism to which she was subjected. His heart went out to her.[16]

Prayer

Use this prayer to help you better organize your own prayer, express your heart more clearly, and think more deeply about God and His Word.

Lord Jesus, as we read about Mary's anticipation of Your death, burial, and resurrection, we thank You that her actions that Saturday night just a week before set a pattern for us. She chose the best she had and focused it on worshiping You. Help us to do the same as we remember all You accomplished on our behalf.

Mary sat at Your feet listening to Your words when You taught. Lord, may we be like that. Thank You that after hearing the prophecy of Your coming death, burial, and resurrection, on this unusual occasion she gave what was valuable—probably a family heirloom—as an act of worship remembering Your death for sin. You said You would give Your life as a ransom for many. She heard and she understood.

Mary recognized her own sin and embraced the reality that she, too, was a sinner in need of a Savior, and she worshiped You for what You were about to accomplish. Father, may our hearts be so inclined toward Your Son. Remind us that the worship of Your Son is our highest priority.

Lord, as we consider the Passion Week, the week that is central in the life of every believer, in human history, and in the eternal plan of redemption, do not let us be distracted by the temporary, the trivial, and the mundane. Rather, help us, O God, to center our hearts on what really matters to You.

Thank You that on the night of His betrayal, even on the morning of His crucifixion, our Lord's robes were still scented with the fragrance of Mary's worship. May we worship Your Son as Mary did.

O, Lord God, open our hearts and minds to understand what Jesus did for us on the cross. Holy Spirit, grant us illumination to understand these realities through Your Word.

We pray in Jesus' name.

Amen.

Response

Write your own prayer based on the same biblical passage and boldly offer it to the God who hears.

The God Who Hears

Day 15

Treasuring the Word of God
2 Timothy 4:1–5

—

Preparation
Ask your heavenly Father to prepare your heart to read and pray His eternal Word.

Scripture Reading
The Word of God reads:

> I solemnly charge you in the presence of God and of Christ Jesus, who is to judge the living and the dead, and by His appearing and His kingdom: preach the word; be ready in season and out of season; reprove, rebuke, exhort, with great patience and instruction. For the time will come when they will not endure sound doctrine; but wanting to have their ears tickled,

they will accumulate for themselves teachers in accordance to their own desires, and will turn away their ears from the truth and will turn aside to myths. But you, be sober in all things, endure hardship, do the work of an evangelist, fulfill your ministry.

Meditation
Deliberately choose to think deeply about what you just read from God's Word. Ask God to grant you illumination so that you can better understand His truth and plan how to practice His truth.

Reflect on Church History
Consider what John Chrysostom (347–407), one of the greatest preachers in the early church, writes about 2 Timothy 4:1–5:

> Therefore, let food, and bathing, and banqueting, and the other necessities of life have a definite time. But let instruction about the love of truth from above have no set hour—let all the time belong to it.[17]

Prayer
Use this prayer to help you better organize your own prayer, express your heart more clearly, and think more deeply about God and His Word.

Father, this passage reminds us that we live in dark and perilous times that are even worse than the first century. Evil men and their false teaching continue to worsen and gather momentum, obscuring the truth, adulterating the gospel, and denying the sufficiency and authority of Your Word. We confess that our hearts are heavy for the professing evangelical church, even for churches around us that have abandoned their confidence in Your Word to pursue other priorities, turning aside from the truth to whatever excites the desires of those who listen.

Lord, we pray that You would help us individually and as a church to do what Paul urges Timothy to do: to place our confidence in the Scriptures. May we remember that it was in Your Word we came to understand the way to know You, the path to Your eternal presence, the means to be forgiven of our sins and made right with You both in time and eternity. Father, it is from the sacred writings we learned these things.

It is Your Word that has continued to equip us for every good work. In our own dark and difficult times, may we be committed to Your Word. Let us not pursue other things or follow those who turn aside from the truth.

O God, give us a growing passion for Your Word, for You have magnified it equal to Your own character. Help us to study it, read it, love it, treasure it, obey it, and pass on its truths to the next generation.

We pray that You would make us faithful until You take us to Yourself or until our Lord returns for us.

We pray it in His magnificent name.

Amen.

Response
Write your own prayer based on the same biblical passage and boldly offer it to the God who hears.

Treasuring the Word of God

Day 16

Redemption in Christ Jesus
Titus 2:11–15

Preparation
Ask your heavenly Father to prepare your heart to read and pray His eternal Word.

Scripture Reading
The Word of God reads:

> For the grace of God has appeared, bringing salvation to all men, instructing us to deny ungodliness and worldly desires and to live sensibly, righteously and godly in the present age, looking for the blessed hope and the appearing of the glory of our great God and Savior, Christ Jesus, who gave Himself for us to redeem us from every lawless deed, and to purify for

Himself a people for His own possession, zealous for good deeds.

These things speak and exhort and reprove with all authority. Let no one disregard you.

Meditation
Deliberately choose to think deeply about what you just read from God's Word. Ask God to grant you illumination so that you can better understand His truth and plan how to practice His truth.

Reflect on Church History
Consider what Matthew Poole (1624–1679), a pastor and theologian, writes about Titus 2:11–15:

> Our great God and Savior Jesus Christ was not only sent and given by the Father but freely gave up himself to be incarnate, and to die for us, *hyper hēmōn*, in our stead to die. "That he might redeem us from all iniquity;" that by that price he might purchase salvation for us, delivering us both from the guilt and power of sin, who were slaves and captives to our lusts.[18]

Prayer
Use this prayer to help you better organize your own prayer, express your heart more clearly, and think more deeply about God and His Word.

Redemption in Christ Jesus

Our Father, as we read these words and reflect on what You have done, we are overwhelmed with Your love for us. Truly, Your grace appeared when Jesus entered our world. We are reminded that You are a God of grace and a Savior by nature. We thank You, O God, for Your grace.

Lord Jesus, as we read this text, we are also reminded that not only did the Father send You into the world, but You volunteered. You, the eternal Son of God, equal with the Father, knowing all it would cost You, took humanity upon Yourself. You became everything we are except for sin.

You came into this world in the womb of a virgin. You were born in the way all of us were born. You lived and walked on this planet just like us. You knew it would cost You thirty quiet, solitary years of living out a life of obedience to Your Father. You knew it would cost You three intense years of ministry when You would give Yourself for Your own, when You would teach and heal, and when You would represent the Father. You knew that for doing so You would be mocked and slandered, questioned about the circumstances of Your birth, and called a servant of Satan himself.

But beyond all that, Lord Jesus, You knew it would cost You the cross. You knew that You were coming to die, that for those dark hours You would endure the wrath of the Father against the sins of everyone who would ever believe in You. You knew that during those lonely hours Your human soul and body would feel the weight of hell itself—what every one of us deserved.

We thank You, Lord Jesus, that You did it for us. You gave Yourself for us to redeem us from every lawless deed—and not merely to forgive us, but to purify for Yourself a people for Your own possession. We acknowledge that we cannot fully grasp the depth of Your love. Help us to remember that it was Your love for us that drove You to such depths.

We pray these things in Your name.

Amen.

Response
Write your own prayer based on the same biblical passage and boldly offer it to the God who hears.

....
....
....
....
....

Redemption in Christ Jesus

Day 17

God's Forgiving and Redeeming Love
Psalm 130

—

Preparation
Ask your heavenly Father to prepare your heart to read and pray His eternal Word.

Scripture Reading
The Word of God reads:

> Out of the depths I have cried to You, O LORD.
> Lord, hear my voice!
>   Let Your ears be attentive
>   To the voice of my supplications.
> If You, LORD, should mark iniquities,
>   O Lord, who could stand?
> But there is forgiveness with You,
>   That You may be feared.

I wait for the LORD, my soul does wait,
> And in His word do I hope.
My soul *waits* for the Lord
> More than the watchmen for the morning;
>> *Indeed, more than* the watchmen
>> for the morning.
O Israel, hope in the LORD;
> For with the LORD there is lovingkindness,
>> And with Him is abundant redemption.
And He will redeem Israel
> From all his iniquities

Meditation
Deliberately choose to think deeply about what you just read from God's Word. Ask God to grant you illumination so that you can better understand His truth and plan how to practice His truth.

Reflect on Church History
Consider what William S. Plumer (1802–1880), a theologian and clergyman, writes about Psalm 130:

> In all the Scriptures we shall not find a sweeter word than redemption. It is a term employed to express the deliverance of men from the misery of captivity, from the hardships of bondage, and from the guilt and wretchedness of a sinful state. All mere men since the fall of Adam have needed redemption.

God's Forgiving and Redeeming Love

> The only Redeemer of God's elect is the Lord Jesus Christ. The ransom paid is not silver or gold or tears or reformations, but the blood of the Son of God.[19]

Prayer

Use this prayer to help you better organize your own prayer, express your heart more clearly, and think more deeply about God and His Word.

Father, like the psalmist we look at ourselves, and find ourselves crying out to You from the depths of our own guilt and sinfulness. We acknowledge we can do nothing to help ourselves. So, we do exactly what the psalmist did: we cry out to You, our gracious and merciful God.

Lord, we can only say, "Hear our voice," because we have nothing that would compel You to hear us except for Your character and Your promise to hear and forgive. So, Lord, hear our voice; let Your ears be attentive to our cries.

Father, if You recorded all our sins—and You do—and if You determined to treat us as those sins deserve, not one of us could stand before You. We would all be swept away from the light of Your presence into the blackness of eternal punishment. But we praise You, O God, and we bless You that there is forgiveness with You that You may be feared.

We are reminded that forgiveness is not something You can offer without cost, because Your justice demands payment for every sin. We thank You that payment was rendered on behalf of all who would ever believe in Jesus our Lord. The price was His life, offered in our place. We thank You for that work of Jesus Christ and for the forgiveness He purchased.

Lord, we love the images You placed in Your Word to picture the fullness of Your forgiveness. You promised to remove our sins as far from us as the east is from the west, to permanently erase them from Your divine records, to hide them behind Your back where You will never see them again, and to bury them in the deepest sea where no one can find them (Ps. 103:12; Isa. 38:17; Mic. 7:19; Acts 3:19).

Father, our souls hope in these promises. Each of us comes seeking this very forgiveness. Out of the depths we cry to You, and we pray You would extend to us the forgiveness purchased in the abundant redemption found in the work of Jesus Christ. Thank You that because You love us with unfailing, steadfast love, You will redeem us from all our iniquities.

We thank You and praise You in Jesus' name.

Amen.

Response

Write your own prayer based on the same biblical passage and boldly offer it to the God who hears.

The God Who Hears

Day 18

The Light of the World
John 12:35–50

Preparation
Ask your heavenly Father to prepare your heart to read and pray His eternal Word.

Scripture Reading
The Word of God reads:

> So Jesus said to them, "For a little while longer the Light is among you. Walk while you have the Light, so that darkness will not overtake you; he who walks in the darkness does not know where he goes. While you have the Light, believe in the Light, so that you may become sons of Light."

> These things Jesus spoke, and He went away and hid

Himself from them. But though He had performed so many signs before them, *yet* they were not believing in Him. *This was* to fulfill the word of Isaiah the prophet which he spoke: "LORD, WHO HAS BELIEVED OUR REPORT? AND TO WHOM HAS THE ARM OF THE LORD BEEN REVEALED?" For this reason they could not believe, for Isaiah said again, "HE HAS BLINDED THEIR EYES AND HE HARDENED THEIR HEART, SO THAT THEY WOULD NOT SEE WITH THEIR EYES AND PERCEIVE WITH THEIR HEART, AND BE CONVERTED AND I HEAL THEM." These things Isaiah said because he saw His glory, and he spoke of Him. Nevertheless many even of the rulers believed in Him, but because of the Pharisees they were not confessing Him, for fear that they would be put out of the synagogue; for they loved the approval of men rather than the approval of God.

And Jesus cried out and said, "He who believes in Me, does not believe in Me but in Him who sent Me. He who sees Me sees the One who sent Me. I have come *as* Light into the world, so that everyone who believes in Me will not remain in darkness. If anyone hears My sayings and does not keep them, I do not judge him; for I did not come to judge the world, but to save the world. He who rejects Me and does not receive My sayings, has one who judges him; the word I spoke is what will judge him at the last day. For I did not speak on My own initiative, but the Father Himself who sent Me has given Me a commandment *as to* what to say and what to speak. I know that His commandment is eternal life; therefore the things I speak, I speak just as the Father has told Me."

Meditation
Deliberately choose to think deeply about what you just read from God's Word. Ask God to grant you illumination so that you can better understand His truth and plan how to practice His truth.

Reflect on Church History
Consider what A. W. Pink (1886–1952), a pastor and theologian, writes about John 12:47:

> Every man who hears the Gospel ought to believe in Christ, and those who do not will yet be punished for this unbelief. As Christ here teaches, the rejector of Him will be judged for his sin. Let any unsaved one who reads these lines thoughtfully ponder this solemn word of the Lord. Jesus.[20]

Prayer
Use this prayer to help you better organize your own prayer, express your heart more clearly, and think more deeply about God and His Word.

Father, we thank You for the Light that You sent into the world. We thank You that He was from You and that the one who has seen Him has seen You (John 14:9). You affirmed Him to be Your own eternal Son when You spoke audibly from heaven and said "This is my beloved Son; listen to Him" (Mark 9:7).

Thank You that You have enabled many to listen to Him, that You opened our blind eyes to see the light of the glory of God in the face of Jesus Christ (2 Cor. 4:6). Lord, it is by Your grace, and Your grace alone, that we have come to know You and to be known by You. We thank You for such grace. We thank You that You have allowed us to know You through the work of Jesus Christ our Lord and have enabled us to see the beauty of the gospel in Him.

But Father, there are many whom we love—members of our families, friends, even our church—who have not seen the light and believed on Him. And in not believing, they have actually rejected Him. We pray that You would open their hearts to see and believe. Help them to see that in the pages of Scripture they have the Light in Jesus Christ. They know who He is—may they believe in Him and in You also, Father (John 14:1).

We pray they would acknowledge that they have taken Your good gifts and prostituted them in the use of sin.

We ask that they would repent of their sins against You and seek Your forgiveness in Jesus Christ. May they believe in the perfect life of Jesus Christ lived in the place of all who would believe in Him, and in His substitutionary death offered to satisfy Your just wrath against individual sins, so that there is no wrath left for us. May they believe in the resurrection of our Lord Jesus Christ as Your own stamp of approval on His perfect work—it truly was finished. Father, may their faith come to rest in Him, and Him alone.

Open our hearts to understand the truth of Your Word. Not just intellectually, but in a way that changes how we think, how we act, and how we live.

We pray this in the name of the One by whom Your light has shone on us, the One who is the Light, our Lord Jesus Christ.

Amen.

Response
Write your own prayer based on the same biblical passage and boldly offer it to the God who hears.

....
....

The God Who Hears

The Light of the World

Day 19

The Grace of God in Salvation
Ephesians 2:1–10

Preparation
Ask your heavenly Father to prepare your heart to read and pray His eternal Word.

Scripture Reading
The Word of God reads:

> And you were dead in your trespasses and sins, in which you formerly walked according to the course of this world, according to the prince of the power of the air, of the spirit that is now working in the sons of disobedience. Among them we too all formerly lived in the lusts of our flesh, indulging the desires of the flesh and of the mind, and were by nature children of

wrath, even as the rest. But God, being rich in mercy, because of His great love with which He loved us, even when we were dead in our transgressions, made us alive together with Christ (by grace you have been saved), and raised us up with Him, and seated us with Him in the heavenly places in Christ Jesus, so that in the ages to come He might show the surpassing riches of His grace in kindness toward us in Christ Jesus. For by grace you have been saved through faith; and that not of yourselves, it is the gift of God; not as a result of works, so that no one may boast. For we are His workmanship, created in Christ Jesus for good works, which God prepared beforehand so that we would walk in them.

Meditation
Deliberately choose to think deeply about what you just read from God's Word. Ask God to grant you illumination so that you can better understand His truth and plan how to practice His truth.

Reflect on Church History
Consider what Ian Hamilton (1950–), a pastor and theologian, writes about Ephesians 2:1–10:

> Sometimes Christians need to be reminded of their past. They need not wallow in it, be crushed by it, or be nostalgic over it, but they should highlight how

blessed and privileged they are in Christ.... It is easy for us to forget what we once were apart from Jesus Christ and the transformation the gospel has accomplished in our lives. When we forget who and what we are in Christ, we slowly lose our sense of love and gratitude to God for His saving love and grace to us in Christ.[21]

Prayer

Use this prayer to help you better organize your own prayer, express your heart more clearly, and think more deeply about God and His Word.

Father, our hearts cry out in response to Your Word: we thank You that Your grace found us out.

Lord, this passage describes us as certainly as it described the believers of the church in Ephesus, and as it described the apostle Paul.

We were dead spiritually, without life, unable to respond to You. We were the "living dead," living out our lives here without any sense of You, our Creator, without any knowledge of You, without any relationship with You. We were in slavery to our sin, to the mindset of the age in which we live—the false religion that permeates this planet—and to Satan himself.

But we thank You, O God, for those two little words: "but God." Because of Your mercy and great love, You found us and extended grace to us. Lord, how can we begin to thank You that there is something in Your character that is so foreign to our own nature (apart from Your grace). It is the quality in Your own great heart that delights and finds joy in doing good to those who deserve exactly the opposite from You. This is our only hope. And it is a magnificent, unwavering hope because it is who You are.

We thank You that You have spiritually rescued us, by Your grace, through the work of Your Son, Jesus Christ. He came to be one of us; Your eternal Son became like us and took upon Himself full and complete humanity, lived a perfect life, and died a substitutionary death: Your Lamb died in our place.

We are Your workmanship, created by You in Christ Jesus, and we give You praise and thanks for Your grace. It truly does amaze us! Help us to cherish this truth. May it never become ordinary or pedestrian. Father, may our minds be controlled every day by this reality, and may we live in the light of it until Christ returns and into the coming ages as You continue to show Your grace and kindness toward us in Him.

For it is in His name we pray.

Amen.

Response
Write your own prayer based on the same biblical passage and boldly offer it to the God who hears.

The God Who Hears

Day 20

The Messiah's Kingdom
Psalm 2

—

Preparation
Ask your heavenly Father to prepare your heart to read and pray His eternal Word.

Scripture Reading
The Word of God reads:

> Why are the nations in an uproar
> > And the peoples devising a vain thing?
>
> The kings of the earth take their stand
> > And the rulers take counsel together
> > > Against the Lord and against
> > > > His Anointed, saying,
>
> "Let us tear their fetters apart
> > And cast away their cords from us!"

The God Who Hears

He who sits in the heavens laughs,
    The Lord scoffs at them.
Then He will speak to them in His anger
    And terrify them in His fury, saying,
"But as for Me, I have installed My King
    Upon Zion, My holy mountain."

"I will surely tell of the decree of the Lord:
    He said to Me, 'You are My Son,
        Today I have begotten You.
'Ask of Me, and I will surely give
    the nations as Your inheritance,
        And the *very* ends of the earth
            as Your possession.
'You shall break them with a rod of iron,
    You shall shatter them like earthenware.'"

Now therefore, O kings, show discernment;
    Take warning, O judges of the earth.
Worship the Lord with reverence
    And rejoice with trembling.
Do homage to the Son, that He not become angry,
    and you perish *in* the way,
        For His wrath may soon be kindled.
            How blessed are all who take refuge in Him!

Meditation

Deliberately choose to think deeply about what you just read from God's Word. Ask God to grant you illumination so that you can better understand His truth and plan how to practice His truth.

Reflect on Church History

Consider what Augustine of Hippo (354–430), an early Church Father, writes about Psalm 2:

> In eternity there is nothing that is past, as though it had ceased to be, nor future, as though not yet in existence; there is present only, because whatever is eternal always is. By this phrase, "today have I begotten you," the most true and catholic faith proclaims the eternal generation of the Power and Wisdom of God, who is the only-begotten Son.[22]

Prayer

Use this prayer to help you better organize your own prayer, express your heart more clearly, and think more deeply about God and His Word.

Our Father, in this magnificent psalm, we are reminded that our world is divided on almost everything except its hatred of You and its antagonism towards Your Son, our Lord Jesus Christ. The world unites to celebrate false religion while despising You and Your loving invitation in the gospel. They see Your all-wise, perfect laws that enable us to lead fulfilling, satisfying lives as enslaving shackles to be torn away rather than loving counsel to be embraced.

Father, we bless You that regardless of the opposition against You and Your Son, You are on Your throne and have determined the outcome of all things. In the end, when man's day is done, You will install Your King, and He will reign on this renewed planet for a thousand years with a rod of iron (Rev. 20:1–6). Any who rebel against Him will be crushed to powder, but all of us whom You have brought to love and serve Him will welcome His loving rule with eagerness and joy.

Lord, we thank You that through the gospel You brought us to acknowledge and accept the sovereign rule of Jesus Christ. It is not hard for us to bow the knee—we do so willingly and gladly, acknowledging that He is Lord, to Your great glory. We thank You that someday every one of Your enemies will also bow the knee and confess that He is Lord (Phil. 2:9–11). Until that day, Father, help us to be faithful to Your calling in our families, our work, our ministries, and the church. Help us to fulfill our duties while we are here and to live in anticipation of the day when You make all things new, when You set everything right, and when Your justice sorts everything out in righteousness and fairness. We praise You that we who deserve the worst from You will forever experience Your grace.

We long for the day when our Lord returns for us. Then He will cleanse this planet during seven years of Tribulation (Rev. 6–19). At the end of those days, He will return in the Second Coming and His feet will stand on the Mount of Olives (Zech. 14:4). He will enter the Great City You determined as the place of His reign, You will install Him as Your King, and we will serve with Him forever.

Lord, may these great truths help us remain centered as we walk through this life, and may we be faithful to Him always.

We pray in His name.

Amen.

Response
Write your own prayer based on the same biblical passage and boldly offer it to the God who hears.

....
....

The God Who Hears

Day 21

Christ's Prayer for His Own
John 17:1–5, 13–26

—

Preparation
Ask your heavenly Father to prepare your heart to read and pray His eternal Word.

Scripture Reading
The Word of God reads:

> Jesus spoke these things; and lifting up His eyes to heaven, He said, "Father, the hour has come; glorify Your Son, that the Son may glorify You, even as You gave Him authority over all flesh, that to all whom You have given Him, He may give eternal life. This is eternal life, that they may know You, the only true God, and Jesus Christ whom You have sent. I glorified

You on the earth, having accomplished the work which You have given Me to do. Now, Father, glorify Me together with Yourself, with the glory which I had with You before the world was."

—

"But now I come to You; and these things I speak in the world so that they may have My joy made full in themselves. I have given them Your word; and the world has hated them, because they are not of the world, even as I am not of the world. I do not ask You to take them out of the world, but to keep them from the evil *one*. They are not of the world, even as I am not of the world. Sanctify them in the truth; Your word is truth. As You sent Me into the world, I also have sent them into the world. For their sakes I sanctify Myself, that they themselves also may be sanctified in truth.

"I do not ask on behalf of these alone, but for those also who believe in Me through their word; that they may all be one; even as You, Father, *are* in Me and I in You, that they also may be in Us, so that the world may believe that You sent Me.

The glory which You have given Me I have given to them, that they may be one, just as We are one; I in them and You in Me, that they may be perfected in unity, so that the world may know that You sent Me, and loved them, even as You have loved Me. Father, I desire that they also, whom You have given Me, be with Me where I am, so that they may see My glory which You have given Me, for You loved Me before the foundation of the world.

"O righteous Father, although the world has not known You, yet I have known You; and these have known that You sent Me; and I have made Your name known to them, and will make it known, so that the love with which You loved Me may be in them, and I in them."

Meditation
Deliberately choose to think deeply about what you just read from God's Word. Ask God to grant you illumination so that you can better understand His truth and plan how to practice His truth.

Reflect on Church History
Consider what George Hutcheson (1615–1674), a Scottish minister and theologian, writes about John 17:

> This chapter contains Christ's solemn prayer to the Father after the farewell sermon, wherein, by supplicating for himself, his disciples, and all his members, he sanctifies the use of prayer to all his

followers, making use of it in his own person for obtaining what he needed. He makes his latter will and testament, leaving his legacies to his followers, and leaves us a pattern of his perpetual intercession in heaven as our great high priest, for upholding ministry in the church, showing what his heart will be in his absence, and what he lives forever to accomplish. He speaks all this openly, in the audience of his disciples, that he may confirm them in the faith of his love, may assure them of what he prays for, and may teach them, by his example, to ask for themselves.[23]

Prayer
Use this prayer to help you better organize your own prayer, express your heart more clearly, and think more deeply about God and His Word.

Our Father, as we read these extraordinary words, we are amazed. We are truly astounded to think that on Thursday night of the Passion Week, as our Lord anticipated the horrific events that would unfold within hours—His arrest, scourging, crucifixion, and His enduring Your divine wrath against our sins—in spite of knowing all those things, His mind and heart were focused on us. He was praying for us. He was concerned about us, His followers, on whom You and He had set Your eternal love.

Lord, we are profoundly grateful for the love You have shown us in Christ. It astounds us as we read this passage that our Lord says You have loved us just as You have loved Him. You loved us though we were once Your enemies (Rom. 5:10). We trampled Your truth underfoot, forsook Your paths, went our own way, and deserved nothing from Your hand. Lord, we praise You that You adopted us as Your own children and now think of us—and treat us—as You treat Your one-of-a-kind, eternal Son. We thank You, Father, for that love.

We thank You, Lord Jesus, that You also loved us with such great love. Before the foundation of the world, You agreed in the eternal counsel of the Trinity that You would come to willingly, voluntarily shoulder our shame and guilt and pay the price.

Father, we confess that we should have suffered and died, but You sent Your precious Son, the Lamb of God, to stand in our place. We thank You and praise You for such love. Help us, O God, to love You in response. May we be known as those who love You and love one another because of the love You have manifested towards us in Christ.

We pray in Jesus' name.

Amen.

Response

Write your own prayer based on the same biblical passage and boldly offer it to the God who hears.

Christ's Prayer for His Own

Day 22

There Is No Other God
Isaiah 45:18-25

Preparation
Ask your heavenly Father to prepare your heart to read and pray His eternal Word.

Scripture Reading
The Word of God reads:

> For thus says the Lord, who created the heavens (He is the God who formed the earth and made it, He established it *and* did not create it a waste place, *but* formed it to be inhabited),

> "I am the Lord, and there is none else.
> "I have not spoken in secret,
> In some dark land;

The God Who Hears

I did not say to the offspring of Jacob,
   'Seek Me in a waste place';
      I, the Lord, speak righteousness,
         Declaring things that are upright.

"Gather yourselves and come;
   Draw near together, you fugitives of the nations;
   They have no knowledge,
      Who carry about their wooden idol
         And pray to a god who cannot save.
"Declare and set forth *your case*;
   Indeed, let them consult together.
      Who has announced this from of old?
      Who has long since declared it?
         Is it not I, the Lord?
           And there is no other
             God besides Me,
                A righteous God and a Savior;
                   There is none except Me.
"Turn to Me and be saved, all the ends of the earth;
   For I am God, and there is no other.
"I have sworn by Myself,
The word has gone forth from
   My mouth in righteousness
      And will not turn back,
         That to Me every knee will bow,
           every tongue will swear *allegiance*.
"They will say of Me,

> 'Only in the Lord are righteousness and strength.'
> Men will come to Him,
> And all who were angry at Him
> will be put to shame.
> "In the Lord all the offspring of Israel
> Will be justified and will glory."

Meditation
Deliberately choose to think deeply about what you just read from God's Word. Ask God to grant you illumination so that you can better understand His truth and plan how to practice His truth.

Reflect on Church History
Consider what J. Alec Motyer (1924–2016), an Old Testament scholar, writes about Isaiah 45:18:

> God is the Creator who had a worldwide people in mind when he created the earth. Four verbs sum up his work: he initiated (created), moulded into shape (fashioned, as a potter would) until all was completed (made) and he imparted stability to the whole (founded). This work of creation proves that he is God (Ps. 96:5) …. When the Lord planned the world he also willed a worldwide people (formed … to be inhabited). It stands to reason therefore that this Creator will have a concern for all his creatures.[24]

Prayer

Use this prayer to help you better organize your own prayer, express your heart more clearly, and think more deeply about God and His Word.

Our Father, we confess with all our hearts the truth of what You have said: the gods of the nations are indeed idols, the work of men's hands that cannot save. You are the only true and living God, who made all things. You formed the earth and stretched out the heavens alone.

We thank You, O God, that You have brought us to understand who You are. You revealed Yourself in Your Word as the great I Am—as Yahweh. And You revealed Yourself ultimately and finally in the Lord Jesus Christ, Your last word to us (Heb. 1:1-2).

We bless You, Father, that You are by nature a saving God. The prophet Isaiah reminds us that there is no other Savior. We cannot save ourselves—from ourselves, from our sin, or the justice our sins deserve before You. We are hopeless without You.

We thank You that You delight to rescue sinners from what they truly deserve. There is no truer measure of Your saving love than our Lord Jesus Christ with His hands stretched out, nailed to a cross. Truly that was the

There Is No Other God

pulpit from which You declared Your love forever! But more than declaring Your love, it was at the cross that You accomplished our redemption, that You accomplished reconciliation between our sinful souls and You, a righteous, holy God (2 Cor. 5:16–21).

Father, we give You thanks that You brought us to understand that in the gospel. And in the gospel, You extended the invitation to us, "Turn to Me and be saved." We were the fugitives of the nations that Isaiah describes. We bless You that You brought us to see and understand the truth about Jesus Christ our Lord: that You sent Him, Your own Son, into the world to live and to die for the sins of all who would believe in Him. You then raised Him from the dead, and now He sits at Your right hand until You make His enemies the footstool of His feet (Ps. 110:1).

This passage reminds us that every person who has ever lived will know our Lord Jesus Christ either as Savior or as Judge. Lord, remind us of this as we interact with those around us. Remind us that if they refuse to bow the knee willingly in this life, acknowledging Him as their Lord, someday they will still bow the knee, acknowledging that He is all He claims, but to their own destruction. Father, give us wisdom and courage to share the gospel. Help our hearts to be filled with Your own passion to see the nations come to know You.

We pray in Jesus' name.

Amen.

Response
Write your own prayer based on the same biblical passage and boldly offer it to the God who hears.

There Is No Other God

Day 23

The Nearness of Yahweh God
Psalm 73

—

Preparation
Ask your heavenly Father to prepare your heart to read and pray His eternal Word.

Scripture Reading
The Word of God reads:

> Surely God is good to Israel,
>   To those who are pure in heart!
> But as for me, my feet came close to stumbling,
>   My steps had almost slipped.
> For I was envious of the arrogant
>   As I saw the prosperity of the wicked.
> For there are no pains in their death,
>   And their body is fat.

The God Who Hears

They are not in trouble *as other* men,
> Nor are they plagued like mankind.

Therefore pride is their necklace;
> The garment of violence covers them.

Their eye bulges from fatness;
> The imaginations of *their* heart run riot.

They mock and wickedly speak of oppression;
> They speak from on high.

They have set their mouth against the heavens,
> And their tongue parades through the earth.

Therefore his people return to this place,
> And waters of abundance are drunk by them.

They say, "How does God know?
> And is there knowledge with the Most High?"

Behold, these are the wicked;
> And always at ease, they have increased *in* wealth.

Surely in vain I have kept my heart pure
> And washed my hands in innocence;

For I have been stricken all day long
> And chastened every morning.

If I had said, "I will speak thus,"
> Behold, I would have betrayed
>> the generation of Your children.

When I pondered to understand this,
> It was troublesome in my sight

The Nearness of Yahweh God

Until I came into the sanctuary of God;
> *Then* I perceived their end.

Surely You set them in slippery places;
> You cast them down to destruction.

How they are destroyed in a moment!
> They are utterly swept away by sudden terrors!

Like a dream when one awakes,
> O Lord, when aroused, You will despise their form.

When my heart was embittered
> And I was pierced within,

Then I was senseless and ignorant;
> I was *like* a beast before You.

Nevertheless I am continually with You;
> You have taken hold of my right hand.

With Your counsel You will guide me,
> And afterward receive me to glory.

Whom have I in heaven *but You*?
> And besides You, I desire nothing on earth.

My flesh and my heart may fail,
> But God is the strength of my heart
>> and my portion forever.

For, behold, those who are far from You will perish;
> You have destroyed all those
>> who are unfaithful to You.

But as for me, the nearness of God is my good;

> I have made the Lord God my refuge,
> That I may tell of all Your works.

Meditation
Deliberately choose to think deeply about what you just read from God's Word. Ask God to grant you illumination so that you can better understand His truth and plan how to practice His truth.

Reflect on Church History
Consider what H. C. Leupold (1892–1972), a Lutheran theologian, writes about Psalm 73:27–28:

> There is nothing more disastrous for man than to let distance intervene between him and his God. Being separated from the source of life, all such "shall perish" .... [But] there is nothing better than to stay with God after one has found Him .... What God has done for him [the psalmist] and what God means to him are matters that he purposes to declare openly so that men may learn to know God and make Him their refuge.[25]

Prayer
Use this prayer to help you better organize your own prayer, express your heart more clearly, and think more deeply about God and His Word.

Our Father, if we are honest with our own hearts and honest before You, we must acknowledge that we at times find ourselves tempted like the psalmist. We look around and see the prosperity of the rich and powerful of our world who are completely wicked and arrogant, even against You, yet they do not seem to face the troubles we face. They have whatever their hearts desire, boasting about their success as if they had accomplished it. Even while they despise and mock You, it seems their power and influence grow and their wealth increases.

Lord, we are sometimes tempted to respond like Asaph, In vain we have kept our hearts pure and washed our hands in innocence. We have been stricken all day long and chastened every morning (cf. v. 13–14). But Father, when we are tempted like this, we come into Your presence and You remind us of the end of the wicked. You remind us of the incredible spiritual wealth that is ours.

Lord, whom have we in heaven but You (cf. v. 25)? Give us Yourself, and there is nothing else we want! You promise to be continually with us, to guide us through this life, just as surely as if You held our hand. You promise to be the strength of our hearts, to be our refuge when we are in trouble. You promise that when this brief life is over, we will enter the glory of Your presence where You plan to lavish us with Your grace forever.

Forgive us, O God, for envying the temporary and fading prosperity of the wicked and for doubting Your ability to reward us, Your children, with true riches. Forgive us for questioning Your wisdom in taking us through trouble, heartache, leanness, and difficulty. And forgive us most of all for having You and wanting anything else! You are our portion forever—and You are all we want!

We are so grateful that You are our God and we are Your people. And we acknowledge that this wonderful New Covenant promise is possible only because of Your Son, who sealed that very covenant with His own blood. Jesus, through His perfect life and substitutionary death and resurrection, made those wonderful promises ours. You are now our God and we are Your people. You have forgiven our sins and will remember them no more, forever (Isa. 43:25; Jer. 31:34; Heb. 8:12).

Father, we thank You for the truth of the gospel, and we thank You that in Christ You have given us Yourself. There is nothing else we want.

We thank You in His name.

Amen.

Response

Write your own prayer based on the same biblical passage and boldly offer it to the God who hears.

The God Who Hears

Day 24

Jesus' Authority to Forgive Sins
Mark 2:1–12

Preparation
Ask your heavenly Father to prepare your heart to read and pray His eternal Word.

Scripture Reading
The Word of God reads:

> When He had come back to Capernaum several days afterward, it was heard that He was at home. And many were gathered together, so that there was no longer room, not even near the door; and He was speaking the word to them. And they came, bringing to Him a paralytic, carried by four men. Being unable to get to Him because of the crowd, they removed the roof

above Him; and when they had dug an opening, they let down the pallet on which the paralytic was lying. And Jesus seeing their faith said to the paralytic, "Son, your sins are forgiven." But some of the scribes were sitting there and reasoning in their hearts, "Why does this man speak that way? He is blaspheming; who can forgive sins but God alone?" Immediately Jesus, aware in His spirit that they were reasoning that way within themselves, said to them, "Why are you reasoning about these things in your hearts? Which is easier, to say to the paralytic, 'Your sins are forgiven'; or to say, 'Get up, and pick up your pallet and walk'? But so that you may know that the Son of Man has authority on earth to forgive sins"—He said to the paralytic, "I say to you, get up, pick up your pallet and go home." And he got up and immediately picked up the pallet and went out in the sight of everyone, so that they were all amazed and were glorifying God, saying, "We have never seen anything like this."

Meditation
Deliberately choose to think deeply about what you just read from God's Word. Ask God to grant you illumination so that you can better understand His truth and plan how to practice His truth.

Reflect on Church History
Consider what J. C. Ryle (1816–1900), an Anglican bishop of

Jesus' Authority to Forgive Sins

Liverpool, writes about Mark 2:1–12:

> Let us consider how great must be the authority of Him, who has the power to forgive sins! This is the thing that none can do but God. No angel in heaven, no man upon earth, no church in council, no minister of any denomination, can take away from the sinner's conscience the load of guilt, and give him peace with God. They may point to the fountain open for all sin. They may declare with authority whose sins God is willing to forgive. But they cannot absolve by their own authority. They cannot put away transgressions. This is the peculiar prerogative of God, and a prerogative which He has put in the hands of His Son Jesus Christ.[26]

Prayer

Use this prayer to help you better organize your own prayer, express your heart more clearly, and think more deeply about God and His Word.

Our Father, we thank You for Your Son, our Lord Jesus Christ. We thank You that in the eternal counsel of Your own being, You decided Your Son would enter this world as one of us. He would continue to be all He had been eternally but would add to Himself full and complete humanity, everything we are except for sin. You determined that as the God-man He would live here among us in perfect obedience to You, and then He would die as the substitute for all who would ever believe in Him (Heb. 2:14–18; 4:15; 5:7–10).

Lord, we are grateful for this snapshot from His life and the powerful lesson it presents. We are amazed at various elements of the story—the faith of this man and his friends and the miracle that a paralyzed man is suddenly able to walk—but what amazes us more is the great spiritual truth to which those elements point: Jesus is not only able to miraculously cure a fractured human body, but He can grant forgiveness and healing to a fractured human soul.

Father, it is such a comfort and encouragement to us who are sinners that You have given Jesus authority on earth to forgive sins. Lord Jesus, we thank You that You have granted us forgiveness. As we read this story, our minds look to the end of Mark's gospel where we see You accomplish our forgiveness by the sacrifice of Yourself. You lay down Your life to satisfy Your Father's justice against us so He could become our Father, our sins could be pardoned, and our fractured souls made whole, as was this man's formerly paralyzed body. We are amazed at such grace.

Jesus' Authority to Forgive Sins

I pray You would help us to think often of these truths and to live in light of them. Help us not only to treasure them ourselves and to adore our Lord, but also to open our mouths to tell others about the authority You gave Him to forgive sins on earth.

We love You and thank You. We pray in the name of the One who purchased our forgiveness, our Lord Jesus Christ.

Amen.

Response
Write your own prayer based on the same biblical passage and boldly offer it to the God who hears.

The God Who Hears

Day 25

Praise the Lord!
Psalm 148

Preparation
Ask your heavenly Father to prepare your heart to read and pray His eternal Word.

Scripture Reading
The Word of God reads:

> Praise the Lord!
>> Praise the Lord from the heavens;
>>> Praise Him in the heights!
>
> Praise Him, all His angels;
>> Praise Him, all His hosts!
>
> Praise Him, sun and moon;
>> Praise Him, all stars of light!
>
> Praise Him, highest heavens,

The God Who Hears

And the waters that are above the heavens!
Let them praise the name of the Lord,
   For He commanded and they were created.
He has also established them forever and ever;
   He has made a decree which will not pass away.

Praise the Lord from the earth,
   Sea monsters and all deeps;
Fire and hail, snow and clouds;
   Stormy wind, fulfilling His word;
Mountains and all hills;
   Fruit trees and all cedars;
Beasts and all cattle;
   Creeping things and winged fowl;
Kings of the earth and all peoples;
   Princes and all judges of the earth;
Both young men and virgins;
   Old men and children.

Let them praise the name of the Lord,
   For His name alone is exalted;
      His glory is above earth and heaven.
And He has lifted up a horn for His people,
   Praise for all His godly ones;
      Even for the sons of Israel, a people near to Him.
         Praise the Lord!

Meditation
Deliberately choose to think deeply about what you just read from God's Word. Ask God to grant you illumination so that you can better understand His truth and plan how to practice His truth.

Reflect on Church History
Consider what David Dickson (1583–1662), Professor of Divinity at Glasgow and Edinburgh, writes about Psalm 148:

> The Lord is glorious in his workmanship and government of all the creatures, but most of all in humankind, whom he calls to be factors, collectors, and chamberlains, as it were, to gather to him the rent of praise and glory from all other creatures, and then to pay praises for their own part also.[27]

Prayer
Use this prayer to help you better organize your own prayer, express your heart more clearly, and think more deeply about God and His Word.

Our Father, our God and King, our Creator and Redeemer, it is right that all creation join in a great symphony of praise to exalt You, its Creator! As we look around and see the magnificence of Your creation, the heavens declare Your glory and all that You have made shows forth Your handiwork (Ps. 19:1).

Lord, we see the vegetation, the animals, and all the inanimate creation, and we are reminded that everything You made exalts Your name as wise, good, and powerful.

But it is reserved for the intelligent creation to praise You as You deserve to be praised. Even now we join our praise to that of the angelic beings gathered in Your presence: the seraphim and cherubim who exalt You and Your holiness, and the angels who are ministering spirits You sent out to do Your bidding (Heb. 1:14) The hosts of heaven exalt You, O God! Even fallen man, though Your image in him is marred almost beyond recognition, brings You praise by virtue of His very existence and the complexity of His being.

But, Lord, it is ultimately those on whom You have set Your love, whom You have called into a relationship with You, for whom You have raised up a horn, a strong Redeemer, and whom You have brought near to You by Your grace—it is reserved for us to praise You as You deserve (Luke 1:69). Yet, our worship seems so weak, so inadequate, so unworthy of You. We long for the day when our moral characters will reflect the beauty of the moral character of Your Son, when our bodies will be like His glorious body, and when we will gather with the hosts of heaven and the redeemed of the ages to worship You perfectly (Rev. 4–5).

Praise the Lord!

Father, until that day, tune our hearts to sing Your praise with all our being.[28] May we exalt and worship You by how we live, how we think, how we speak, and the testimony we bear to Your truth. May we worship You as the Almighty God until the day we stand in Your presence and worship You perfectly.

We praise You and thank You in the name of our Lord Jesus Christ.

Amen.

Response
Write your own prayer based on the same biblical passage and boldly offer it to the God who hears.

....
....
....
....
....
....
....
....
....
....
....

The God Who Hears

Day 26

The Righteousness of Christ
Philippians 3:1–11

—

Preparation
Ask your heavenly Father to prepare your heart to read and pray His eternal Word.

Scripture Reading
The Word of God reads:

> Finally, my brethren, rejoice in the Lord. To write the same things *again* is no trouble to me, and it is a safeguard for you.

> Beware of the dogs, beware of the evil workers, beware of the false circumcision; for we are the *true* circumcision, who worship in the Spirit of God and

glory in Christ Jesus and put no confidence in the flesh, although I myself might have confidence even in the flesh. If anyone else has a mind to put confidence in the flesh, I far more: circumcised the eighth day, of the nation of Israel, of the tribe of Benjamin, a Hebrew of Hebrews; as to the Law, a Pharisee; as to zeal, a persecutor of the church; as to the righteousness which is in the Law, found blameless.

But whatever things were gain to me, those things I have counted as loss for the sake of Christ. More than that, I count all things to be loss in view of the surpassing value of knowing Christ Jesus my Lord, for whom I have suffered the loss of all things, and count them but rubbish so that I may gain Christ, and may be found in Him, not having a righteousness of my own derived from the Law, but that which is through faith in Christ, the righteousness which comes from God on the basis of faith, that I may know Him and the power of His resurrection and the fellowship of His sufferings, being conformed to His death; in order that I may attain to the resurrection from the dead.

Meditation
Deliberately choose to think deeply about what you just read from God's Word. Ask God to grant you illumination so that you can better understand His truth and plan how to practice His truth.

Reflect on Church History
Consider what John Calvin (1509–1564), a French Reformer, writes about Philippians 3:10:

> He points out the efficacy and nature of faith—that it is the knowledge of Christ, and that, too, not bare or indistinct, but in such a manner that the power of his resurrection is felt. *Resurrection* he employs as meaning, the completion of redemption, so that it comprehends in it at the same time the idea of death. But as it is not enough to know Christ as crucified and raised up from the dead, unless you experience, also, the fruit of this, he speaks expressly of efficacy. Christ therefore is rightly known, when we feel how powerful his death and resurrection are, and how efficacious they are in us. Now all things are there furnished to us—expiation and destruction of sin, freedom from condemnation, satisfaction, victory over death, the attainment of righteousness, and the hope of a blessed immortality.[29]

Prayer
Use this prayer to help you better organize your own prayer, express your heart more clearly, and think more deeply about God and His Word.

Our Father, as we read these words, we are so grateful for

Your work in the heart of the apostle Paul. We thank You that You brought him to this understanding, that You snatched him from the darkness of his self-righteousness and gave him the light of the glory of Jesus Christ and the gospel.

We are also reminded that You have done the same for us. Lord, we thank You that there was a time when You brought us to see the utter worthlessness of our own righteousness, to realize that we had nothing we could offer You and no way to earn Your favor. As You did with Paul, and with every true believer, You reduced us to beggars, crying for Your mercy and grace in Christ Jesus (Luke 18:13–14). We thank You that You not only showed us our sin, but also the glory and beauty of Jesus Christ, even as You showed Paul that day on the road to Damascus when he saw the risen Lord (Acts 9:1–19). In the past, we used the name of Jesus only to curse. We ignored Him. We did not esteem Him. But You brought us to see the value of knowing Christ Jesus our Lord and, in light of knowing Him, everything else became like refuse. You caused us to see that our only hope was a righteousness outside of ourselves: His righteousness, "His robes for mine: O wonderful exchange!"[30]

We thank You, Lord, that in Your wisdom You brought us to know and understand the gospel, and to know Christ.

The Righteousness of Christ

Our desire, like Paul's, is to know Him better, to grow in our understanding of His life, death, and resurrection, and eventually to be raised to new life with Him—to share the body of His glory, and to be in His presence forever.

Father, help us to live seeing Christ, loving Christ, serving Christ, following Christ, and anticipating Christ.

We pray it in His name.

Amen.

Response
Write your own prayer based on the same biblical passage and boldly offer it to the God who hears.

....
....
....
....
....
....
....
....
....
....

The God Who Hears

Day 27

The Servant of Yahweh
Isaiah 42:1–9

—

Preparation
Ask your heavenly Father to prepare your heart to read and pray His eternal Word.

Scripture Reading
The Word of God reads:

> "Behold, My Servant, whom I uphold;
>> My chosen one *in whom* My soul delights.
>>> I have put My Spirit upon Him;
>>>> He will bring forth justice to the nations.
>
> "He will not cry out or raise His *voice*,
>> Nor make His voice heard in the street.
>
> "A bruised reed He will not break
>> And a dimly burning wick He will not extinguish;

The God Who Hears

He will faithfully bring forth justice.
"He will not be disheartened or crushed
    Until He has established justice in the earth;
        And the coastlands will wait
            expectantly for His law."

Thus says God the LORD,
    Who created the heavens and stretched them out,
        Who spread out the earth and its offspring,
            Who gives breath to the people on it
                And spirit to those who walk in it,
"I am the Lord, I have called You in righteousness,
    I will also hold You by the hand and watch over You,
        And I will appoint You
            as a covenant to the people,
                As a light to the nations,
To open blind eyes,
    To bring out prisoners from the dungeon
        And those who dwell in darkness
            from the prison.
"I am the Lord, that is My name;
    I will not give My glory to another,
        Nor My praise to graven images.
"Behold, the former things have come to pass,
    Now I declare new things;
        Before they spring forth I proclaim *them* to you."

Meditation
Deliberately choose to think deeply about what you just read from God's Word. Ask God to grant you illumination so that you can better understand His truth and plan how to practice His truth.

Reflect on Church History
Consider what J. A. Alexander (1809–1860), a professor at Princeton Seminary, writes about Isaiah 42:8:

> The general doctrine of the verse is that true and false religion cannot co-exist; because, however tolerant idolatry may be, it is essential to the worship of [Yahweh] to be perfectly exclusive of all other gods. This is included in the very name [Yahweh], and accounts for its solemn proclamation here.[31]

Prayer
Use this prayer to help you better organize your own prayer, express your heart more clearly, and think more deeply about God and His Word.

Our great God and Father, we bless You that You are a God who lives, who knows, who speaks. You can predict the future because You have prescribed it. Father, we worship You as the great, all-knowing Yahweh, the One who simply is. And we thank You, O God, that 700 years before our Lord came, You caused these words to be written through the prophet Isaiah. Thank You for this prophecy of our Lord Jesus Christ and all that was fulfilled in His earthly ministry.

Thank You that You sent Him to proclaim the gospel, to accomplish the gospel, and to ensure that the gospel is personally applied. He came to open blind eyes, literally and spiritually, and to bring prisoners in slavery and in darkness out from the dungeon of their sins. To them He brought light and salvation (1 Pet. 2:9).

Father, we thank You that He was compassionate with those who, like bruised reeds, were cast off and unwanted. They came humbly to Him and He did not break them. Instead, He repaired their lives and restored them. Those whose lives were like a dimly burning, nearly extinguished candle He did not put out. Instead, through the power of His Spirit, He breathed fresh life, and those smoldering wicks burst into flames.

O God, we thank You that He still does this today and that many of us have experienced His salvation. He has opened our blind eyes. He has set us free from the dungeon of our slavery to sin. He has made us right with You through His own life and death and resurrection.

We bless You for the gospel and for Your Servant, Your

Anointed One, the Messiah who came, Jesus Christ our Lord. We thank You also that He will come again, and when He does, He will not stop until He establishes justice on the earth among the nations. We know a day is coming when, for the first time in our lives, we will experience the rule of a just, wise, gracious, compassionate King. To those who submit to Him He will show the same compassion He demonstrated in His first coming. Those who rebel, He will crush with a rod of iron (Ps. 2:9).

Father, we thank You that the day is coming when Jesus Christ our Lord will reign on this planet. Until then, help us to be faithful and to live in anticipation of His coming.

We pray in Jesus' name.

Amen.

Response
Write your own prayer based on the same biblical passage and boldly offer it to the God who hears.

....
....
....
....
....

The God Who Hears

Day 28

The New Birth
John 3:1–17

Preparation
Ask your heavenly Father to prepare your heart to read and pray His eternal Word.

Scripture Reading
The Word of God reads:

> Now there was a man of the Pharisees, named Nicodemus, a ruler of the Jews; this man came to Jesus by night and said to Him, "Rabbi, we know that You have come from God *as* a teacher; for no one can do these signs that You do unless God is with him." Jesus answered and said to him, "Truly, truly, I say to you, unless one is born again he cannot see the kingdom of God."

Nicodemus said to Him, "How can a man be born when he is old? He cannot enter a second time into his mother's womb and be born, can he?" Jesus answered, "Truly, truly, I say to you, unless one is born of water and the Spirit he cannot enter into the kingdom of God. That which is born of the flesh is flesh, and that which is born of the Spirit is spirit. Do not be amazed that I said to you, 'You must be born again.' The wind blows where it wishes and you hear the sound of it, but do not know where it comes from and where it is going; so is everyone who is born of the Spirit."

Nicodemus said to Him, "How can these things be?" Jesus answered and said to him, "Are you the teacher of Israel and do not understand these things? Truly, truly, I say to you, we speak of what we know and testify of what we have seen, and you do not accept our testimony. If I told you earthly things and you do not believe, how will you believe if I tell you heavenly things? No one has ascended into heaven, but He who descended from heaven: the Son of Man. As Moses lifted up the serpent in the wilderness, even so must the Son of Man be lifted up; so that whoever believes will in Him have eternal life.

"For God so loved the world, that He gave His only begotten Son, that whoever believes in Him shall not perish, but have eternal life. For God did not send the Son into the world to judge the world, but that the world might be saved through Him."

Meditation
Deliberately choose to think deeply about what you just read from God's Word. Ask God to grant you illumination so that you can better understand His truth and plan how to practice His truth.

Reflect on Church History
Consider what Gregory of Nazianzus (c. 329–390), a Cappadocian Church Father, writes about John 3:

> And indeed from the Spirit comes our new birth, and from the new birth our new creation, and from the new creation our deeper knowledge of the dignity of him from whom it is derived.[32]

Prayer
Use this prayer to help you better organize your own prayer, express your heart more clearly, and think more deeply about God and His Word.

Our Father, these amazing words have resonated through the centuries since our Lord spoke them. We thank You for the reminder of Your sovereignty in salvation. Your Spirit is like the wind: He blows wherever He wills, and He brings life where He chooses.

We thank You that He accomplishes salvation through the new birth, as our Lord describes here. Through His power, through the Word heard, understood, and applied to the heart, He makes us new in Christ. We were born all over again: redeemed, regenerated, and given new desires and affections.

Thank You that You sent Your own Son to accomplish this on our behalf. You so loved the world of mankind that You sent Your one-of-a-kind, unique Son to become like us, while still retaining His complete deity. He took on Himself the full humanity each of us has, and He lived among us like one of us. He lived a perfect life—a life of perfect obedience to Your law.

It staggers our minds, O God, having lived as long as we have and sinned as often as we have, to think of One who never sinned once in thought, in word, or in act. He then laid down that perfection, that perfect life, in our place. For those dark hours on the cross, You poured out Your anger and wrath on our sins so You could forgive us (Mark 15:33). You were separated from Him during that time so we could enjoy Your presence forever. Father, we thank You that whoever believes in Him, as many of us have, "shall not perish, but have eternal life."

We bless You and thank You for the redemption that is found in, and through, our Lord Jesus Christ, in whose name we pray.

Amen.

Response
Write your own prayer based on the same biblical passage and boldly offer it to the God who hears.

Day 29

The Intercession of Jesus Christ
1 Peter 1:1–9

—

Preparation
Ask your heavenly Father to prepare your heart to read and pray His eternal Word.

Scripture Reading
The Word of God reads:

> Peter, an apostle of Jesus Christ,
>
> To those who reside as aliens, scattered throughout Pontus, Galatia, Cappadocia, Asia, and Bithynia, who are chosen according to the foreknowledge of God the Father, by the sanctifying work of the Spirit, to obey Jesus Christ and be sprinkled with His blood: May grace and peace be yours in the fullest measure.

Blessed be the God and Father of our Lord Jesus Christ, who according to His great mercy has caused us to be born again to a living hope through the resurrection of Jesus Christ from the dead, to *obtain* an inheritance *which is* imperishable and undefiled and will not fade away, reserved in heaven for you, who are protected by the power of God through faith for a salvation ready to be revealed in the last time. In this you greatly rejoice, even though now for a little while, if necessary, you have been distressed by various trials, so that the proof of your faith, *being* more precious than gold which is perishable, even though tested by fire, may be found to result in praise and glory and honor at the revelation of Jesus Christ; and though you have not seen Him, you love Him, and though you do not see Him now, but believe in Him, you greatly rejoice with joy inexpressible and full of glory, obtaining as the outcome of your faith the salvation of your souls.

Meditation
Deliberately choose to think deeply about what you just read from God's Word. Ask God to grant you illumination so that you can better understand His truth and plan how to practice His truth.

Reflect on Church History
Consider what Matthew Henry (1662–1714), a minister and theologian, writes about 1 Peter 1:2:

By the Father we are here to understand the first person of the blessed Trinity. There is an order among the three persons, though no superiority; they are equal in power and glory, and there is an agreed economy in their works. Thus, in the affair of man's redemption, election is by way of eminency ascribed to the Father, as reconciliation is to the Son and sanctification to the Holy Spirit, though in each of these one person is not so entirely interested as to exclude the other two. Hereby the persons of the Trinity are more clearly discovered to us, and we are taught what obligations we are under to each of them distinctly.[33]

Prayer

Use this prayer to help you better organize your own prayer, express your heart more clearly, and think more deeply about God and His Word.

Father, we rejoice in the salvation that is ours. We thank You along with Peter as we read these magnificent words describing how we were chosen by You in eternity past according to Your great foreknowledge. You set us apart unto Yourself by the work of the Spirit to this great end: that we who have been saved would obey Jesus Christ since we have been sprinkled with His blood, cleansed and forgiven through His sacrifice in our place.

Certainly, Father, we join Peter in blessing You, the God and Father of our Lord Jesus Christ, because it is by Your great mercy that You caused us to be born again. You gave us new spiritual life. We were dead to You, to everything good and to everything spiritual, but You gave us life through Your Word and Spirit unto a living hope.

We live not merely for what we enjoy in this life, but for what You have promised in the life to come. We thank You that throughout our days here we live with joy, though at the same time we are distressed, grieved by various trials and troubles in this life. We know that You are using them for our good, and that You are protecting us through this life.

We thank You that though we have not physically seen Jesus Christ with our eyes, we love Him because You brought us to see Him as He is in Scripture. Though we do not see Him yet, we still believe in Him. Our faith is unwavering because of Your work and the work of Your Spirit, and as we ponder the weight of glory that awaits us, we greatly rejoice with joy that cannot even be expressed.

Father, give us endurance as we run this race (Heb. 12:1–2). Give us perseverance in our faith (Rom. 5:3–5). Lord, preserve, protect, and defend us that You may present us faultless in Your presence with exceeding joy. To You, the only wise God (Rom. 16:27), we give our praise and glory and honor, even as we will when Jesus comes and we see Him face to face.

It is in His name we pray.

Amen.

Response
Write your own prayer based on the same biblical passage and boldly offer it to the God who hears.

The God Who Hears

Day 30

No Other Name
Acts 3:13–21; 4:5–12

Preparation
Ask your heavenly Father to prepare your heart to read and pray His eternal Word.

Scripture Reading
The Word of God reads:

> "The God of Abraham, Isaac and Jacob, the God of our fathers, has glorified His servant Jesus, *the one* whom you delivered and disowned in the presence of Pilate, when he had decided to release Him. But you disowned the Holy and Righteous One and asked for a murderer to be granted to you, but put to death the Prince of life, *the one* whom God raised from the dead,

a fact to which we are witnesses. And on the basis of faith in His name, *is* the name of Jesus which has strengthened this man whom you see and know; and the faith which *comes* through Him has given him this perfect health in the presence of you all.

"And now, brethren, I know that you acted in ignorance, just as your rulers did also. But the things which God announced beforehand by the mouth of all the prophets, that His Christ would suffer, He has thus fulfilled. Therefore repent and return, so that your sins may be wiped away, in order that times of refreshing may come from the presence of the Lord; and that He may send Jesus, the Christ appointed for you, whom heaven must receive until *the* period of restoration of all things about which God spoke by the mouth of His holy prophets from ancient time."

—

On the next day, their rulers and elders and scribes were gathered together in Jerusalem; and Annas the high priest *was there*, and Caiaphas and John and Alexander, and all who were of high-priestly descent. When they had placed them in the center, they *began to* inquire, "By what power, or in what name, have you done this?" Then Peter, filled with the Holy Spirit, said to them, "Rulers and elders of the people, if we are on trial today for a benefit done to a sick man, as to how this man has been made well, let it be known to all of you and to all the people of Israel, that by the name of Jesus Christ the Nazarene, whom you crucified, whom God raised from the dead—by this *name* this man stands here before you in good health. He is the STONE WHICH WAS REJECTED by you, THE BUILDERS, *but* WHICH BECAME THE CHIEF CORNER *stone*. And there is salvation in no one else; for there is no other name under heaven that has been given among men by which we must be saved."

Meditation
Deliberately choose to think deeply about what you just read from God's Word. Ask God to grant you illumination so that you can better understand His truth and plan how to practice His truth.

Reflect on Church History
Consider what John Gill (1697–1771), a Baptist pastor and theologian, writes about Acts 4:12:

> God resolved in his purposes and decrees, in his council and covenant, upon the salvation of his chosen people; and he appointed his Son to be the salvation of them, and determined he would save them by him, and by no other, and in no other way; wherefore, whoever are saved, must be saved by him.[34]

Prayer

Use this prayer to help you better organize your own prayer, express your heart more clearly, and think more deeply about God and His Word.

God, we thank You for the clarity of the apostle Peter. We thank You that Your Spirit stirred him and spoke through him, and we thank You for his message (2 Pet. 1:20–21). We thank You for our Lord Jesus Christ. You raised Him up. You sustained Him through His life and ministry, and You put Him to death as a sacrifice for sins, using the sinful hands of men without being tainted by their sin (Acts 2:22–23; 4:27–28). Thank You for raising Him from the dead on the third day.

As we read these words of the apostle Peter, we are overwhelmed with gratitude that You brought us to see and understand these things. It is entirely Your doing that we have come to embrace the exclusivity of Jesus Christ as the only way to be right with You, the one true and living God. Lord, this is not of us: we are pluralists and self-righteous by nature. We thank You that You brought us to embrace the truth found only in Jesus Christ Your Son. We affirm and confess that there is no other name under heaven that You have given to us by which we can be spiritually rescued.

Lord, that is Your mercy and sovereign grace toward us. We would never have come to that understanding on our own. We would never have turned from our sin had You not worked in our hearts. We would never have confessed that Jesus Christ is Lord if You had not, by Your Spirit, enabled us to do so. And, Father, as we stand firm as worshipers of You through Your Son, Jesus Christ, we give You alone the praise.

Help us to understand Jesus' sacrifice more clearly and to love Him more deeply. May our hearts be captivated by the life, death, and resurrection of Your Son and the salvation freely offered in Him.

We pray in Jesus' name.

Amen.

Response
Write your own prayer based on the same biblical passage and boldly offer it to the God who hears.

....
....
....
....
....

The God Who Hears

Day 31

The Coming of the Son of Man
Daniel 7:9–14

—

Preparation
Ask your heavenly Father to prepare your heart to read and pray His eternal Word.

Scripture Reading
The Word of God reads:

> "I kept looking
> > Until thrones were set up,
> > > And the Ancient of Days took His seat;
> > > > His vesture *was* like white snow
> > > > > And the hair of His head like pure wool.
> > > > > > His throne *was* ablaze with flames,
> > > > > > > Its wheels *were* a burning fire.

"A river of fire was flowing
    And coming out from before Him;
        Thousands upon thousands
            were attending Him,
                And myriads upon myriads
                      were standing before Him;
                The court sat,
                      And the books were opened.

"Then I kept looking because of the sound of the boastful words which the horn was speaking; I kept looking until the beast was slain, and its body was destroyed and given to the burning fire. As for the rest of the beasts, their dominion was taken away, but an extension of life was granted to them for an appointed period of time.

"I kept looking in the night visions,
    And behold, with the clouds of heaven
        One like a Son of Man was coming,
            And He came up to the Ancient of Days
            And was presented before Him.
"And to Him was given dominion,
    Glory and a kingdom,
        That all the peoples,
            nations and *men of every* language
                Might serve Him.

> His dominion is an
> everlasting dominion
> Which will not pass away;
> And His kingdom is one
> Which will not
> be destroyed."

Meditation
Deliberately choose to think deeply about what you just read from God's Word. Ask God to grant you illumination so that you can better understand His truth and plan how to practice His truth.

Reflect on Church History
Consider what Philipp Melanchthon (1497–1560), a German Reformer, writes about Daniel 7:

> God makes known great things from the beginning: the advent of his Son, the future judgment, the resurrection of the dead, the eternal punishment of the wicked, the eternal glory of believers and the exact succession or order of kingdoms before the final judgment. God did not reveal these things in vain but that his will would be carefully considered. And, indeed, this doctrine taught Daniel and others about eternal life and the future judgment.... We know with certainty that this doctrine, which Daniel professed, is divine, and we will not allow it to be taken away from us.[35]

Prayer
Use this prayer to help you better organize your own prayer, express your heart more clearly, and think more deeply about God and His Word.

Our Father, we are so comforted by the reality that You are the Ancient of Days, the eternally wise, all-powerful One. You are the One who holds court—and nothing stands in Your way. You make decisions, and they are carried out.

Father, thank You that while our world rages in a state of upheaval and turmoil, You experience nothing but peace and calm. We find great joy in the reality that You are in absolute, complete, sovereign control of everything that happens on this earth, even that day in the future when the most wicked ruler of all will exert his power over this planet. You are unmoved, unchanged, and Your purpose will be accomplished.

We rejoice that You have always had a plan—a plan centered in the Person of Your Son, our Lord Jesus Christ. All history focuses on Him. We divide the pages of world history based on His first coming: His coming to be one of us, to live among us, to die for sins, to purchase the forgiveness of His people, and to ascend into Your presence.

The Coming of the Son of Man

O God, we thank You that all human history is building toward His Second Coming, when He will come in glorious might to take back His world and end its night. You have told us the day is coming when You will give Him a kingdom. It will not be like the kingdoms of our world, that come onto the stage of history and shortly pass from it. Rather, You will establish a kingdom for Him that will never be destroyed. We thank You that we will reign with Him for a thousand years on this very planet after it is renewed. Then He will destroy all creation and make a new heaven and a new earth in which righteousness dwells (2 Pet. 3:13). We are profoundly grateful for the certainty of our future.

Father, we acknowledge that You also control our individual lives and all that unfolds: all that has already occurred and all that will come. Lord, every day, hour, and moment of our lives You have orchestrated and mapped out for Your own great purposes: for the exaltation of Your Son, our Lord Jesus Christ, and the glory of Your great name.

We bow our hearts before Your throne. Help us, O Lord, to trust You more.

We pray in Jesus' name.

Amen.

Response

Write your own prayer based on the same biblical passage and boldly offer it to the God who hears.

The Coming of the Son of Man

Endnotes

1 Day 1 · Titus 3:1–8
Day 2 · Psalm 65
Day 3 · Hebrews 10:11–25
Day 4 · Revelation 21:22–22:7
Day 5 · Psalm 23
Day 6 · Luke 14:25–33
Day 7 · Matthew 1:18–25
Day 8 · Job 19:23–29
Day 9 · 1 Corinthians 15:1–8
Day 10 · Psalm 104:1–23
Day 11 · Ephesians 3:14–21
Day 12 · Romans 3:9–20
Day 13 · 2 Thessalonians 2:13–17
Day 14 · Mark 14:3–9
Day 15 · 2 Timothy 4:1–5
Day 16 · Titus 2:11–15
Day 17 · Psalm 130
Day 18 · John 12:35–50
Day 19 · Ephesians 2:1–10
Day 20 · Psalm 2
Day 21 · John 17:1–5, 13–26
Day 22 · Isaiah 45:18–25
Day 23 · Psalm 73
Day 24 · Mark 2:1–12
Day 25 · Psalm 148
Day 26 · Philippians 3:1-11
Day 27 · Isaiah 42:1–9
Day 28 · John 3:1–17
Day 29 · 1 Peter 1:1–9
Day 30 · Acts 3:13–21; 4:5–12
Day 31 · Daniel 7:9–14

2 John Chrysostom, cited in 2 Peter Gorday, ed., *Colossians, 1–2 Thessalonians, 1–2 Timothy, Titus, Philemon*, Ancient Christian Commentary on Scripture (Downers Grove, IL: InterVarsity Press, 2000), 304.

3 David Dickson, *Psalms*, Geneva Series of Commentaries (Carlisle, PA: Banner of Truth, 2021), 379.

4 Martin Luther, cited in Ronald K. Rittgers and Timothy George, eds., *Hebrews, James: New Testament*, vol. XIII, Reformation Commentary on Scripture (Downers Grove, IL: IVP Academic, 2017), 141.

5 John F. MacArthur Jr., *Revelation 12–22*, MacArthur New Testament Commentary (Chicago: Moody Press, 2000), 288.

6 Augustine of Hippo, cited in Craig A. Blaising and Carmen S. Hardin, eds., *Psalms 1–50*, Ancient Christian Commentary on Scripture (Downers Grove, IL: InterVarsity Press, 2008), 180.

7 Leon Morris, *Luke: An Introduction and Commentary*, Tyndale New Testament Commentaries 3 (Downers Grove, IL: InterVarsity Press, 1988), 254.

8 George Beverly Shea, "I'd Rather Have Jesus" (Word Music, LLC., 1967).

9 J. C. Ryle, *Expository Thoughts on Matthew* (New York: Robert Carter & Brothers, 1860), 6.

10 Charles H. Spurgeon, "I Know that My Redeemer Lives," taken from The Metropolitan Tabernacle Pulpit C. H. Spurgeon Collection, Sermon 504, Spurgeon Gems, https://www.spurgeongems.org/sermon/chs504.pdf.

11 Philipp Melanchthon, cited in Scott M. Manetsch, Timothy George, and David W. McNutt, eds., *1 Corinthians: New Testament*, vol. IXa, Reformation Commentary on Scripture (Downers Grove, IL: IVP Academic, 2017), 351.

12 George Horne, *Commentary on the Psalms* (Audubon, NJ: Old Path Publications, 1997), 444.

13 Charles Hodge, *A Commentary on the Epistle to the Ephesians* (New York: Robert Carter and Brothers, 1858), 192.

14 F. F. Bruce, *Romans: An Introduction and Commentary*, vol. 6, Tyndale New Testament Commentaries (Downers Grove, IL: InterVarsity Press, 1985), 103.

15 Heinrich Bullinger, cited in Lee Gatiss, Bradley G. Green, and Timothy George, eds., *1-2 Thessalonians, 1-2 Timothy, Titus, Philemon: New Testament*, vol. XII, Reformation Commentary on Scripture (Downers Grove, IL: IVP Academic, 2019), 99.

16 William Hendriksen, *Exposition of the Gospel According to Mark*, New Testament Commentary (Grand Rapids: Baker, 1975), 561.

17 John Chrysostom, cited in Peter Gorday, ed., *Colossians, 1–2 Thessa-*

lonians, 1–2 Timothy, Titus, Philemon, Ancient Christian Commentary on Scripture (Downers Grove, IL: InterVarsity Press, 2000), 271.

18 Matthew Poole, cited in Lee Gatiss, Bradley G. Green, and Timothy George, eds., 1-2 Thessalonians, 1-2 Timothy, Titus, Philemon: New Testament, vol. XII, Reformation Commentary on Scripture (Downers Grove, IL: IVP Academic, 2019), 294.

19 William S. Plumer, Studies in the Book of Psalms: Being a Critical and Expository Commentary, with Doctrinal and Practical Remarks on the Entire Psalter (Philadelphia; Edinburgh: J. B. Lippincott Company; A & C Black, 1872), 1125.

20 Arthur Walkington Pink, Exposition of the Gospel of John (Swengel, PA: Bible Truth Depot, 1923–1945), 695.

21 Ian Hamilton, Ephesians, ed. Joel R. Beeke and Jon D. Payne, The Lectio Continua Expository Commentary on the New Testament (Grand Rapids, MI: Reformation Heritage Books, 2017), 61.

22 Augustine of Hippo, cited in Craig A. Blaising and Carmen S. Hardin, eds., Psalms 1–50, Ancient Christian Commentary on Scripture (Downers Grove, IL: InterVarsity Press, 2008), 14–15.

23 George Hutcheson, cited in Christopher Boyd Brown, ed., John 13–21, vol. V, Reformation Commentary on Scripture (Downers Grove, IL: IVP Academic, 2021), 114.

24 J. Alec Motyer, Isaiah: An Introduction and Commentary, vol. 20, Tyndale Old Testament Commentaries (Downers Grove, IL: InterVarsity Press, 1999), 327–328.

25 H. C. Leupold, Exposition of the Psalms (Grand Rapids: Baker, 1959), 531.
26 J. C. Ryle, Expository Thoughts on Mark (London: William Hunt, 1859), 29–30.
27 David, Dickson, cited in Herman J. Selderhuis and Timothy George, eds., Psalms 73–150: Old Testament, vol. VIII, Reformation Commentary on Scripture (Downers Grove, IL: IVP Academic, 2018), 392.
28 Robert Robinson and John Wyeth, "Come, Thou Fount of Every Blessing," Repository of Sacred Music (1813).

29 John Calvin, *Commentaries on the Epistles of Paul the Apostle to the Philippians, Colossians, and Thessalonians* (Bellingham, WA: Logos Bible Software, 2010), 98.

30 Chris Anderson and Greg Habegger, "His Robes for Mine" (Church Works Media, 2008).

31 J. A. Alexander, *Commentary on Isaiah* (Grand Rapids: Kregel, 1992), 138.

32 Gregory of Nazianzus, cited in Joel C. Elowsky, ed., John 1–10, Ancient Christian Commentary on Scripture (Downers Grove, IL: InterVarsity Press, 2006), 110.

33 Matthew Henry, Commentary on 1 Peter 1:2

34 John Gill, Commentary on Acts 4:12

35 Philipp Melanchthon, cited in Carl L. Beckwith, Timothy George, and Scott M. Manetsch, eds., *Ezekiel, Daniel: Old Testament*, vol. 12, Reformation Commentary on Scripture (Downers Grove, IL: IVP Academic, 2012), 342–343.

About the Author

Tom Pennington has served as Pastor-Teacher at Countryside Bible Church in Southlake, Texas since 2003. Prior to arriving in Texas, Tom served in various roles at Grace Community Church in Sun Valley, California for 16 years. His ministry at Grace included being an elder, Senior Associate Pastor, and the personal assistant to John MacArthur. Tom was also an adjunct faculty member of The Master's Seminary and served as Managing Director of *Grace to You*.

In addition to his pastoral role at Countryside, he serves as Dean of the Dallas Distance Location at The Master's Seminary, teaches various seminary courses, and is actively involved internationally in training pastors in expository preaching.

Tom's preaching and teaching ministry at Countryside is featured on *The Word Unleashed* (thewordunleashed.org).

Books by Tom Pennington

Jesus' High View of Scripture

The Biblical View of Abortion*

God's Sermon on His Name

A Biblical Case for Cessationism*

Three Hallmarks of a Biblical Church Member*

The God Who Hears

All the World's a Stage

Faithful Stewards

The Pastor and Systematic Theology

From Rome to Reformation*

Christ's Plan for the Church

Exercising the Right Kind of Leadership

Being the Right Kind of Leader

A Biblical Case for Elder Rule

Preaching in the Spirit's Power

Loving Christ by Leading His Sheep

The Shepherd on His Knees

Purchase at
thewordunleashed.org

Also available in Spanish

The Word Unleashed

The Word Unleashed is a ministry of Countryside Bible Church in Southlake, Texas, featuring the Sunday morning and evening preaching of Pastor-Teacher Tom Pennington. Our aim is to make available, through various means and platforms, Tom's expository sermons of the inspired, inerrant, authoritative Word of God.

—

Exalting God's Glory. Explaining God's Truth.

—

thewordunleashed.org
Facebook
X
Instagram
YouTube
Apple Podcasts
Spotify